Bureaucratic Opposition

(PPS-12)

Pergamon Titles of Related Interest

Comfort—*Evaluation and Effectiveness of Public Policy Education*

Gartner—*Consumer Education in the Human Services*

Geismar—*Families in an Urban Mold*

Mushkin & Dunlop—*Health: What Is It Worth? Measures of Health Benefits*

PERGAMON
POLICY
STUDIES

Bureaucratic Opposition

Challenging Abuses at the Workplace

Deena Weinstein

Pergamon Press

NEW YORK • OXFORD • TORONTO • SYDNEY • FRANKFURT • PARIS

Pergamon Press Offices:

U.S.A. Pergamon Press Inc., Maxwell House, Fairview Park, Elmsford, New York 10523, U.S.A.

U.K. Pergamon Press Ltd., Headington Hill Hall, Oxford OX3 0BW, England

CANADA Pergamon of Canada Ltd., 150 Consumers Road, Willowdale, Ontario M2J 1P9, Canada

AUSTRALIA Pergamon Press (Aust) Pty. Ltd., P O Box 544, Potts Point, NSW 2011, Australia

FRANCE Pergamon Press SARL, 24 rue des Ecoles, 75240 Paris, Cedex 05, France

FEDERAL REPUBLIC OF GERMANY Pergamon Press GmbH, 6242 Kronberg/Taunus, Pferdstrasse 1, Federal Republic of Germany

Library of Congress Cataloging in Publication Data

Weinstein, Deena.
    Bureaucratic opposition.

    (Pergamon policy studies)
    Includes bibliographical references and index.
    1. Industrial relations. 2. Bureaucracy.
3. Organizational behavior. I. Title.
HD6971.W42   1978   301.18'32   78-27772
ISBN 0-08-023903-X
ISBN 0-08-023902-1 pbk.

Printed in the United States of America

To Michael, who actualized Heideggerian freedom

Contents

Preface

It is in the interest of those who control the bureaucratic organizations in contemporary societies to have their employees, their clients, and the general public believe that such organizations are purely administrative entities. The myth of administration defines organizations as efficient and effective instruments for the realization of publicly proclaimed goals. All too often social scientists have accepted the idea of pure administration and used it as the basis of their analyses of bureaucracies. Even when they have challenged claims of efficiency and effectiveness, they have not attended to phenomena that contradict the very possibility of an administrative entity. Most of the neglected phenomena involve political processes such as conflict, domination, abuse of power, and deception, which are ubiquitous in organizations. Although disputes over goals, policies, and their implementation are not supposed to occur outside of proper "channels" they arise continually in daily bureaucratic life. Their neglect by social scientists shows a bias, often unintentional, in favor of elite perspectives, and this has perpetuated a distorted and one-dimensional image of organizations. A critical interpretation, which is the aim of this study, does not take official definitions at their face value and does not merely argue in favor of a "conflict approach," but demonstrates concretely the political dimension of activity within bureaucracies.

This book is an attempt to show that contemporary bureaucratic organizations are not only administrative entities but are also political structures in the sense that power, conflict, and domination are normal within them. The specific means used to demonstrate this general thesis is the study of oppositions to administrative authority by subordinates whose activity is not officially legitimate. Bureaucratic opposition is unequivocally political and its occurrence refutes the myth that organizations are merely instruments to achieve externally prescribed goals efficiently and effectively. The study of such oppositions shows how organizations "go wrong" according to their own criteria and how employees become political actors, and so transcend their roles.

Making bureaucratic oppositions a focus for inquiry can be viewed as an

ix

PREFACE

extension of the current research in organizational analysis, which began more than 40 years ago, directed to revealing the "informal" dimensions of behavior within bureaucracies. The studies of informal groups and networks of rules have, for the most part however, stressed adaptive mechanisms and have kept the officially defined context intact. Informal mechanisms are not direct challenges to authority, although they often serve to make authority bearable. Bureaucratic oppositions do, in part, challenge the authority structure and show that the myth of administration cannot be upheld. Reactions to them by officials clearly demonstrate that the organization is, among other things, a power system.

This study not only has links to a tradition in organizational analysis, but is also part of a wider project aimed at revealing the ubiquity of political processes in contemporary complex societies. Hence, it should be interpreted in conjunction with the author's work on the political dimensions of the sociology of knowledge, the critique of the myth of the "scientific community," and the general critique of functionalism. (1) The basic intent of this body of work is to show that underneath the claims of value neutrality, public service, disinterestedness, and good intentions made by apologists for institutional elites lies a world of political conflict and competition. Bringing this world to view is one of the tasks of criticism, which is an intellectual preparation for freedom.

The method implicit in this study might best be called "ethico-empirical." The assumption is made that social existence is an uneasy synthesis of the conflict among interests and the appeal to principles or moral grounds (ideals). Ideals cannot be reduced to interests, as the positivists claim, nor can interests be reduced to ideals, as the idealists contend. No conceptual synthesis of the "material" and "ideal," is possible whether on Marxism, Hegelian, or even Parsonian (dualistic) grounds. The best that can be done is to try to detect the interplay of the two dimensions in actual cases, in much the way that Max Weber, Georg Simmel, and C. Wright Mills attempted to do. The results of such an investigation will not fit a systems model or a "flow chart," but they will not lack coherence. That coherence, however, will not be linear, but will reveal a dialectic between transcendence of partial interest and subservience to such interest. It will not suggest any middle term or mediation between what Kant called "inclination" and "duty." Keeping this distinction clear is the essence of what Kant meant by criticism applied to social life. This study, then, draws upon many cases of opposition which illustrate concretely the tension between principle and interest, and show the paradoxes and ambiguities of political struggle.

The plan of this work follows its critical aim and its ethico-empirical method. The first chapter outlines the myth of neutral administration and proposes the alternative political interpretation of organizations, drawing upon contemporary thought and research on oppositions in the polity. Chapter 2 systematically details the grounds or "good reasons" for oppositions, their normative justifications. The third and fourth chapters add the "empirical" dimension, detailing the barriers that oppositions confront in getting underway and the strategies that they employ once they have been initiated. Chapter 5 analyzes some of the responses to oppositions by the official hierarchy and discusses some of the policies that have been proposed to eliminate the abuses uncovered by dissidents or to "institutionalize" dissent. Hence, the design of the work defines a "process" of opposition, beginning with the circumstantial and normative bases for politics in bureaucracies, and then considering the initiation, methods, and consequences of oppositions. The identification of a process, with various phases, dictated the decision to draw upon case material to illustrate general statements rather than to draw general statements from exhaustive case descriptions. This does not mean, however, that the method is "deductive" rather than "inductive." Whether case material is used illustratively or exhaustively there is always a reciprocity in actual research between general statements and particular data.

Many people have helped to bring this project to completion, whether or not they were aware of giving such assistance. I am grateful to my students at De Paul University, graduates and undergraduates, who informed me about the particulars of the bureaucratic oppositions in which they or those close to them took part. Long after courses were completed some of these students, especially Ms. Edie Zukauskas, continued their interest in my project, discussing it and doing further research in the area. Many of my colleagues in the social science disciplines have been kind enough to speak with me about the general issue of politics within organizations and about bureaucratic oppositions. It was in discussions with Fred Homer that the idea of bureaucratic opposition first arose. I am indebted to him and to Larry Spence, Marie Haug, James Stever, Arthur Kroker, and Robert Perrucci. Finally, this book could not have been written were it not for the active, sympathetic, and intelligent collaboration of my colleague Dr. Michael Weinstein. I cannot thank him enough, and fortunately he does not demand such gratitude.

NOTE

(1) See, for example: Deena Weinstein and Michael A. Weinstein, Living Sociology: A Critical Introduction, New York: David McKay, 1974; Deena Weinstein, "Determinants of Problem Choice in Scientific Research," Sociological Symposium #16 (Summer 1976): 13-23; Deena Weinstein and Michael A. Weinstein, "Sociologies of Knowledge as Rhetorical Strategies," Free Inquiry 16, #1 (May 1978): 1-14; and Deena Weinstein and Michael A. Weinstein, "The Sociology of Non-knowledge: A Paradigm," in R.A. Jones, ed., Research in Sociology of Knowledge, Sciences and Art: An Annual Compilation, Greenwich, Connecticut: J.A.I. Press, 1978, pp. 151-166.

1 Bureaucratic Oppositions: The Phenomenon

> As long as the world shall last there will be wrongs, and if no man objected and no man rebelled, those wrongs would last forever.
>
> - Clarence S. Darrow in an address to the jury at a Communist Trial, Chicago, 1920 (quoted by Arthur Weinberg, Attorney for the Damned, New York: Simon and Schuster)

What do the following accounts have in common?

The regional sales manager of a prominent book publisher advocated various forms of bribery to get professors to adopt his company's textbooks. To demonstrate one of his techniques, he and a subordinate entered a professor's office and asked his judgment of their introductory text. The professor unceremoniously told them that he thought the book was terrible. This professor, however, was in charge of mass sections of the introductory course in his discipline, so, without missing a beat, the sales manager offered him a deal. If he adopted the text for the fall, the manager would send him 400 free copies which could be sold to students at a profit of over $2,000. The professor decided to assign the book to his students.

At sales meetings the manager asked each of his staff members to discuss their "creative" means of selling, that is, the kinds of bribes that they offered and how they proffered them. All of the salesmen were opposed to such methods and preferred to seek adoptions by appealing to the merits of their books. When the manager continued to insist on his methods, five of the six salesmen sent a letter to the main office of the corporation, threatening to resign collectively if their supervisor was not dismissed. The manager was not fired, however, but merely admonished. For several months he kept a low profile and then vigorously renewed his efforts to have his subordinates use his sales techniques. Within the ensuing half year all of the salesmen resigned. Shortly afterwards their supervisor was dismissed.

1

In a large metropolitan school district in which the students scored below average on standardized examinations, a principal of one of the elementary schools directed his teachers specifically to teach the contents of the exams and to increase each pupil's test grade by several points. The teachers feared informing the administrators in the Board of Education because of two possible reprisals: they might be transferred to a school in a "bad" neighborhood or such formal rules as having to turn in a lesson plan book each week might be enforced against them. They did, however, secretly inform the local P.T.A. and helped the parent's group draft a letter to the Board of Education exposing the principal. The Superintendent sent an investigating team, composed of six other principals, to the school. The principal was not fired and continued to try to implement his policies.

Frank Serpico's story, which was made into an interesting movie and an uninspired television series, is widely known. Serpico, a police officer in New York City, wanted to put an end to the rampant corruption in the Department. First he attempted to speak to high-level administrators, but discovered that some of them were involved in the very activities that he was trying to curb. The other administrators took no action. When he broadened his campaign by seeking aid from politicians he was similarly frustrated:

...he was repeatedly rebuffed in his efforts to get action from high police and political officials, continually risking discovery at any moment by the crooked cops he rubbed shoulders with every day, and finally out of desperation... he went to a newspaper with his story. (1)

What do these three accounts or the numerous others that could have been cited in their stead have in common? They all relate attempts to change a bureaucracy by those who work within the organization but who do not have any authority.   These attempts, which will be called "bureaucratic oppositions," are probably ubiquitous, but are not frequently discussed in social science literature for reasons that will be elaborated. Most people who have worked in a large organization for several years are familiar with at least one instance similar to the ones described above, and every so often the press will make such a case public.

It is significant that there has previously been no term in the literature of social science that identified bureaucratic oppositions. This phenomenon has occurred frequently in both private and public organizations, and has been perpetrated by one person or small groups, utilizing any of a number of tactics and meeting with a wide range of outcomes.   These attempts at change from below, which emanate from those who lack authority, are labeled bureaucratic oppositions because they occur outside the normal administrative routine and are challenges to authority. However, their aim is not to usurp the machinery of power but to alter practices and personnel. Why has bureaucratic opposition, a common phenomenon in organizations, been ignored by students of the organization?   In essence, contemporary organization theories screen out this phenomenon by the limitations of their guiding concepts.

The idea of theory in social science that guides the present discussion is at variance with the common-sense notion that facts are immediate perceptions of an objective world which spontaneously generate theories when they are properly related. The actual process of theorizing is the reverse of common sense: the concepts that make up our theories direct us to some phenomena and exclude our attention to others. Metaphorically, theories are beams of light forming an intellectual spectrum that allows us to "see" certain things while leaving others imperceptible. (2) Other beams bring a different selection of facts to light and do not make apparent another, residual, set. The assumption is that no beam covers the entire spectrum; indeed, that different beams have varying band widths which cover distinct portions of the full spectrum. The phenomenon of bureaucratic opposition, then, is identified by a particular theoretical perspective which is quite different from the dominant perspective in contemporary organization studies, for which this phenomenon is all but invisible. A brief description of the currently dominant perspective and its limitations will precede an analysis of the alternative view, within which bureaucratic opposition can be understood.

Although there are many variations on the theme, prevailing theories of organizations are essentially based on a "rational model" which explains "organizational patterns - social structures, motivational strategies, coordinating mechanisms, etc. as outcomes of a goal-seeking or need-fulfilling tendency of the organization." (3) One of the ways in which theories "discover" facts is by directing inquiry to a specific problem. In the case of the prevailing organizational analyses, the problems explored are those of top management and the perspective generated is the manager's.

That is, research questions have been posed from the standpoint of a powerful actor concerned with the essentially technical adjustments necessary to enhance the effectiveness of the organization. (4)

The bias of most organization theory towards the cares and concerns of particular actors within the object of study has often resulted in descriptions of bureaucracies that do not so much reflect the complexity of the total situation as they express the managerial vision of what "ought" to exist. Supporting this contention, Randall Collins claims that spanning a 30 year period the "neo-rationalist line of managerial theory from Chester Barnard (1938) to James D. Thompson (1967) ... is designed as a practical guide for managers as well as a general theory." (5)

Max Weber's ideal-typical description of the bureaucratic organization has been the model imitated by contemporary organization theory. The features of Weber's construct, such as a hierarchy of authority, hiring and promotion based on competence, and specific and written duties for each organizational role, can be summed up by the term rationalization. This concept identifies the process by which instrumental rationality, in which the means to an end are related according to the criterion of efficiency in a predictable pattern of cause and effect, becomes the overriding principle of social activity. In the ideal of a rationalized organization, decisions are made by those at the peak of the hierarchy of authority in the name and interests of constituencies such as citizens or stockholders. These decisions are then implemented efficiently by subordinates. Organizations are interpreted as tools for accomplishing ends, and so the human beings composing them are primarily interpreted as means and not as ends-in-themselves.

Much of the theory and research concerning organizations concentrates on the impediments to maximum efficiency and centers on how management might overcome the irrationality of workers, whose informal groups may reinterpret the rules, and their own misunderstandings of workers. C. Wright Mills concludes that the managerial perspective assumes "the classic formulae of a natural harmony of interests," efficient coordination which, from time to time, is "interfered with by the frailty of human relations, as revealed by the unintelligence of managers and the unhappy irrationality of workmen." (6) Conflict, when acknowledged at all, is usually subsumed under the concept of disorganization. As such it is interpreted as being irrationally motivated and inimical to the ends of the organization, both substantive and technical.

The bias of conventional organization theory, which excludes phenomena evincing conflict, is paralleled by the efforts of organizational elites to eliminate conflict. For both organization theory and managerial ideology, action is divided into two categories. Rational action corresponds to the bureaucratic ideal in which orders flow down the hierarchy of authority and obedience follows, enhancing efficiency. As Weber puts it: "The official is entrusted with specialized tasks and normally the mechanism cannot be put into motion or arrested by him, but only from the very top." (7) The second category of action, which is really residual, is labeled irrational and is defined as all behavior inimical to the efficient attainment of organizational goals. Maintaining this false dichotomy, organization theorists fail to recognize as rational activity whatever does not emanate from the hierarchy of authority.

In a broader sense than the organization theorists use it, rationality may refer to the use of appropriate means to solve a problem, to reach a goal. In this sense the rationality of an action is evaluated according to its adequacy to the actor's goal. The fallacy underlying the false dichotomy in managerial theories of organization is that of referring all action to the goals of upper-level management, and thereby taking an ideological or partial perspective as the basis of scientific theory. Thus, when subordinates disobey orders or attempt to change policies, the managerial theorists view their actions as irrational because of assumptions that 1) those in authority know and order appropriate means to reach universally shared goals and 2) there is agreement on the goals themselves, whether they be efficiency, profit or, more usually, subgoals which are simply means to other ends. Both these assumptions of managerial theory are utterly unwarranted.

It is little wonder, then, that those holding the assumptions of managerial theory would fail to recognize bureaucratic oppositions, which are essentially rational activities that challenge the validity of one or both these assumptions. Belief in shared goals and rational management perpetuates a myth of organizations as systems of purely administrative activity. Criticism of these assumptions discloses another view of organizations in which they appear as semi-congeries of administrative activity interlarded with political processes. Those perspectives which do not acknowledge political activity, then, can neither observe nor name the phenomenon of bureaucratic opposition.

The perspective guiding the present discussion includes the administrative or managerial interpretation of the organization within it, defining administration as a special case of political processes. Where there is complete agreement on or acceptance of goals and procedures and their implementation, organizations are merely administrative entities in which there are no grounds for opposition or dissent but subjective will or emotion (irrationality). Of course, such agreement is hardly ever present in an organization, and so if there is no overt opposition one may assume that it is suppressed by fear, resignation, or prudence, the grounds for reluctant obedience to authoritarian regimes. Only in the case of perfect agreement is Lenin's dictum that politics be reduced to administration realized. Curent organization theory rests on the myth of administration, and systematically ignores phenomena contradictory to that myth.

The administrative myth contains its own interpretation of the human condition or what Alvin Gouldner has called domain assumptions. Talcott Parsons, who applied the managerial viewpoint to contemporary society, makes these domain assumptions. He "defines the human being as an organism seeking short-range pleasures, which must be controlled and directed to sacrifice these desires for the maintenance of collective projects. These collective projects, mediated through organizations, result in providing the conditions for the survival of the organism. The person who holds such a conception of human nature believes that human beings need religion, the nation, the family, the state, and corporate economic enterprises to save them from their own tendencies toward self-indulgence, self-destruction, and the destruction of others." (8)

In contrast to managerial theory, the domain assumptions of the present discussion, which support the idea that organizations are political systems, interpret human beings as purposive actors who have the potential to act on motives that are not rooted in fear, resentment, or selfish enjoyment, and who are sometimes able to question the prevailing "definition of the situation" and to act on their critical insight. The dominant value of this perspective is neither control nor instrumental rationality, but the freedom of the person as a moral actor, which is not factual but must be achieved through struggle. Bureaucratic oppositions, whether they are successful or not, are consistent with the motive of freedom, if only the negative freedom of eliminating some perceived abuse. The perspective guiding this discussion does not deny the existence of the motivations identified by Parsons, but balances them with the freedom of the autonomous moral person.

In summary, the basic contention of the political perspective on organizations is that administrative action is not capable of encompassing all of the activities within an organization because 1) all goals and sub-goals are not shared (that is, there is disagreement about whether certain goals should be pursued) and 2) administrators do not always act "rationally" (that is, those in managerial roles do not always conduct themselves in accordance with universal criteria). (9) Organizations, then, are not fully rationalized: instrumental rationality, in which the means to an end are related as steps in a predictable pattern of cause and effect, is limited by other human processes. Where work is not totally machine-like and so routine that the laborers are merely extensions of the tools that they use, there are possibilities for different interpretations of what should be done, what aspects of the occupational role should be emphasized, what constitutes justice with regard to rewards and punishments, and when decisions about work become commentaries on the worth and dignity of the worker.

The political perspective on organizations developed here draws upon Karl Mannheim's distinction between routine and political activity. According to Mannheim there are two aspects of any social situation: "first, a series of social events which have acquired a set pattern and recur regularly; and, second, those events which are still in the process of becoming, in which, in individual cases, decisions have to be made that give rise to new and unique situations." (10)   The advantage of Mannheim's distinction is that political activity is not identified with coercion or with any other technique of social control but, instead, with uncertainty, diversity, and dispute. Mannheim was mistaken, however, when he identified routinization with rationality and politics with irrationality, arguing approvingly that the "chief characteristic of modern culture is the tendency to include as much as possible in the realm of the rational and to bring it under administrative control - and, on the other hand, to reduce the 'irrational' element to the vanishing point." (11) In contrast to Mannheim's position, the present discussion is based on the notion that political disputes are not "irrational" at all, but reflect, primarily, disagreement on the criteria for evaluating goals.   To say that political activity is "irrational" is to imply that it is possible to achieve a universal agreement on goals merely by perfecting means.

Except for those parts of production organizations in which the role definition of the blue-collar worker is relatively unambiguous and programmed by machinery and other tools, and in which opposition to the possibly immoral consequences of production is excluded by the terms of the "contract," organizations are pervious to political processes. For example, much activity within organizations relates to people as clients, subordinates, or the public. In the modern cultures of the West there has been a tendency to distinguish between the realms of things and persons (Kant's differentiation of the phenomenal world from the "kingdom of ends" is perhaps the most lucid example), each realm having its distinctive standards. Organizations which, for the most part, interpret human beings as means rather than as ends-in-themselves provide many occasions for their morally sensitive employees to dispute policies, and even overall goals. Further, even where there is agreement on principles, those who handle "claims" or "cases" are interpreting systems of rules and are likely to have their own "judicial ideologies" which may clash with those of their superiors. Finally, above the middle-level of organizational hierarchies, politics is inevitable because at these upper levels decisions are made concerning routines. Logically, such decisions cannot themselves be routine and there may be conflict over alternative policies and disagreement about whether a particular decision was "right" or "in the best interests" of the agency or sub-unit.

Political activity in organizations is also precipitated when promotion and firing, as well as working conditions (for example, scheduling in hospitals or academic institutions), are not routinized according to specific procedures. Competition for preferment, attempts at undermining rivals, and resentment at being passed over are not bureaucratic oppositions, but may encourage, lead to, or deepen them. Attempts to make things seem as though they are routine or that they are determined by "objective" standards of efficiency or productivity are essentially rhetorical strategies which, like the managerial viewpoint, have the political import of minimizing challenges to authority.

Traditionally, politics has been interpreted as the aspect of human activity in which decisions are made about such issues as the proper definition of function, policy, and justice. Politics has meant the possibility of choosing among alternatives within a public situation; hence, discretion and the possibility for varying interpretations are essential aspects of political relations. Economic or instrumental activity can be programmed; this is not the case for political activity in which contradictory values may be at stake. We are concerned here with bureaucratic oppositions, which have been defined as attempts to change organizations from within by those who lack the authority to make such changes. Organizational policy and personnel can also be opposed by those who are outside the organization, such as clients, consumers, or anyone affected by the organization including the public at large, as evidenced by environmentalist groups. The study of opposition to organizations from the outside is an important part of the study of bureaucracies as political systems, but it is the subject of another investigation than the one undertaken here.

The political process, whether it occurs in the state or in a bureaucratic organization, involves opposition when some members of an authority system do not acquiesce in decisions that have been made, in the procedures for making them, or in their implementation. With regard to opposition, the essential structural difference between authority systems is whether they have institutionalized procedures for dissent or have not recognized the legitimacy of dissent. Representative systems, in the contemporary world democratic states, institutionalize dissent by allowing for "loyal" oppositions which do not violate constitutional procedures, while authoritarian systems do not make such provisions. Most complex organizations have an authoritarian structure, or at least severely limit representative decision making, and so oppositions within them will be more similar to those in authoritarian states than to those in democracies.

There is a good case, then, for drawing analogies between bureaucratic oppositions and oppositions to authoritarian states. Although a corporation does not have absolute authority over a given geographical area as does a state, both are systems of authoritative decision making which do not officially acknowledge opposition. Employees, like citizens of authoritarian regimes, lack freedoms:

... no freedom of speech - if they gave their subordinates or the press details on the incompetence of their board they would be liable to be fired, and if this is not the death penalty, it can still shatter (one's) life as much as banishment; no right of trial, and no judiciary which is independent of the executive - their career can be blighted and promotion stopped for utterly unjust reasons ... and they have no sort of representation in the councils which decide how the firm shall be run, no say in its government, however much the decisions may affect their lives. (12)

The Chairman of the Board of Sears, Roebuck, and Company concurs:

> ... we complain about the totalitarian state, but in our individual
> organizations ... we have created more or less of a totalitarian system
> in industry, particularly in large industry. (13)

The strategies and tactics of oppositions, both against states and organizations, vary according to circumstances and are not definitive of the phenomenon of opposition itself. Contemporary political scientists, for example, often differentiate between violent and nonviolent oppositions. At the violent end of the continuum are internal wars. An internal war is defined by Eckstein as "any resort to violence within a political order to change its constitution, rulers, or policies." (14)   Under this concept he subsumes revolution, civil war, revolt, rebellion, uprising, guerilla warfare, mutiny, jacquerie, coup d'etat, terrorism, and insurrection. According to Kornhauser, who is specifically concerned with rebellion, such processes are "alternatives to established ways of making demands on authority in an orderly manner ... ways of performing political functions in the absence of political structures capable of accommodating political demands." (15) Such alternatives, of course, need not be violent, and there are many types of nonviolent opposition to both authoritarian and formally democratic states, ranging from clandestine disobedience to public and principled "civil disobedience" such as that advocated by Thoreau.

Bureaucratic oppositions are usually nonviolent because of the state's monopoly of force, although where the organization is a repository of this force (for example, a police department) conflict may become violent. Most bureaucratic oppositions use the tactics of dissenting groups in entrenched authoritarian states, such as clandestine informal organization, symbolic protest, publicity, appeal to higher authority, and, when possible, manipulation of procedures. In many respects, bureaucratic oppositions are similar to the nonviolent protests of dissidents in contemporary Eastern European states.

A political perspective on organizations not only directs attention to the previously neglected phenomenon of bureaucratic oppositions but also opens up the resources of political science for organizational studies. Oppositions within the polity, particularly revolutions but also rebellions, other internal wars, and protest movements, have been extensively studied. A review of some of the pertinent categories and conclusions of the political science literature is useful for providing analogies, parallels, and contrasts between oppositions in the polity and those in bureaucracies. Such comparison also is an aid to understanding the nature of political processes in a more general sense than that attainable when interest is focused exclusively on the institution of the state.

The host of oppositional movements within the polity have been distinguished from one another on the basis of purpose and strategy. Revolutions aspire to a total alteration in the socio-political system.

> Revolutionary change is aimed initially at the political/governmental
> machinery. In this sense political revolution involves a power transfer,
> a change in the distribution of political power, a transformation of the

ruling class. ... This power transformation aims at, seeks, or sets the stage for broader social change. Political revolution entails an array of disruptions on all fronts: political, economic, psychological, social. (16)

Less drastic and total forms of opposition than revolution are aimed at changing certain policies and/or replacing particular personalities. Thus, rebellions, coups, and civil disobedience, for example, are reformist rather than revolutionary. Bureaucratic oppositions are necessarily reformist, because a revolutionary opposition in an organization would presuppose transforming the social structure in which the organization was embedded or using the organization to transform that structure. While opposition intended to use the organization as a revolutionary weapon is not only possible but occurs in cases of "infiltration," such opposition does not seek to transform the organization in order to improve it but merely to use it. Bureaucratic oppositions, then are generally both nonviolent and reformist, and are parallel to similar oppositions within authoritarian states.

A subsidiary distinction refers to the scope of opposition. Some oppositions are pursued within the boundaries of the organization or the polity, and others attempt to draw aid from outside. The "human rights" policy of President Carter, which arose partly in response to the appeals of dissidents in various authoritarian states, is an instance of nonviolent oppositions in some polities gaining support from another political system. "Whistle blowing," in which a dissident member of an organization seeks the aid of communications media or governmental institutions, is a case of bureaucratic oppositions going "outside," widening the scope of conflict.

The preceding distinctions among the strategies, aims, and scopes of oppositional activity both in the polity and the organization will provide the general categorical framework for the chapters to follow. Other distinctions from the political science literature, such as those referring to leadership, the conditions for opposition, and the stages of oppositional activity will be introduced, clarified, criticized, and adapted where they are appropriate. Further elucidation of the practice and problems of bureaucratic opposition will be provided by many examples. These examples have been collected in various ways and should not be viewed as necessarily representative of all such cases. The "universe," as statisticians call it, of all bureaucratic oppositions is unknown, and possibly unknowable. Many of the examples have been gleaned from the mass media, while others originated from non-random interviews with people who work within organizations, including my students. Interestingly enough, no one who had been employed in a large bureaucracy for more than a year was unaware of at least one bureaucratic opposition and many had participated in one or more struggles. Rather than proceeding inductively, the examples will be used to illustrate generalizations derived from theory about bureaucratic oppositions. Attention will first be directed to the causes, conditions, and settings within which bureaucratic oppositions arise. Second, the processes and problems of opposition group formation - from the overcoming of "habits of obedience" to risk, trust, and leadership - will be examined. An exploration of the various strategies and tactics of oppositions will precede an evaluation of their prospects, outcomes, and significance.

CHAPTER 1: NOTES

(1) Peter Mass, Serpico, New York: Bantam, 1973, p. 11.

(2) For a defense of the relativity of fact to perspective, see Jean-Paul Sartre's Search for a Method, New York: Random House, 1963, in which he develops the notion of totalization.

(3) J. Kenneth Benson, "Innovation and Crisis in Organizational Analysis," Sociological Quarterly 18, #1 (Winter, 1977): p.3.

(4) Ibid. p.4.

(5) Randall Collins, Conflict Sociology, New York: Academic Press, 1976, p. 296.

(6) C. Wright Mills, The Sociological Imagination, New York: Oxford University Press, 1958, p. 92.

(7) Max Weber, "Bureaucracy," in From Max Weber: Essays in Sociology, pp. 196-244, H.H. Gerth and C. Wright Mills (eds.), New York: Oxford University Press, 1946, p. 228.

(8) Michael A. Weinstein, "Against Human Nature," Paper delivered at the meetings of the Midwest Political Science Association, Chicago, 1974, p. 9.

(9) The political perspective is not the only possible alternative to the managerial view. For some others, including negotiated order and Marxist perspectives on the organization, see J. Kenneth Benson (ed.), Sociological Quarterly, 18, #1 (Winter, 1977) and especially Wolf Heydebrand's contribution to that number, "Organizational Contradictions in Public Bureaucracies: Toward a Marxian Theory of Organizations," 83-107.

(10) Karl Mannheim, Ideology and Utopia, New York: Harcourt, Brace and World, 1936, pp. 112-113.

(11) Ibid., p. 114.

(12) Anthony Jay, Management and Machiavelli: An Inquiry into the Politics of Corporate Life, New York: Bantam Books, 1968, pp. 16-17.

(13) Ralph Nader, Peter J. Petkas and Kate Blackwell (eds.), Whistle Blowing: The Report on the Conference on Professional Responsibility. New York: Grossman Publishers, 1972, p. xiii.

(14) Harry Eckstein, "On the Causes of Internal Wars," in Eric A. Nordlinger (ed.), Politics and Society: Studies in Comparative Political Sociology. Englewood Cliffs: Prentice-Hall, 1970, pp. 287-88.

(15) William Kornhauser, "Rebellion and Political Development," in Harry Eckstein (ed.), Internal War: Problems and Approaches. New York: The Free Press, 1964, p. 142.

(16) Mostafa Rejai, The Strategy of Political Revolution. Garden City: Doubleday, 1973, p. 8.

2 Grounds for Bureaucratic Opposition

The greatest of faults, I should say, is to be conscious of none.
- Thomas Carlyle, <u>Heroes and Hero Worship</u>

Organizations are fields for political activity, not the purely administrative entities that are described by their apologists and elites. They differ from democratic political structures, however, because, like authoritarian states, they do not have institutionalized oppositions. Organizations do not have routine procedures for the expression and implementation of the demands, or proposals for change, issuing from those who are intimately affected by them but do not have formal authority. Attempts to effectuate change from below, to influence the circumstances within the organization in which one is employed, necessitate initiative, energy, and risk-taking beyond the voting and letter writing that characterize most participation in mass democracies. In subsequent chapters the kinds of initiative, risk taking, and strategy guiding bureaucratic opposition will be discussed. In the present chapter the preliminary issue of why people take such extraordinary measures within their organizations will be addressed. Why are bureaucratic oppositions undertaken? What are the reasons why people overcome inertia, which is supported by the managerial myth, and come to believe that they might and should struggle for change?

The question of why bureaucratic oppositions are undertaken is ambiguous. In the contemporary social sciences the reasons for a phenomenon are normally interpreted to be efficient causes, the observable conditions antecedent to the appearance of the phenomenon. However, there is another meaning of "why" in accounts of human activity which refers to final causes, the legitimate grounds or justifications for a certain kind of conduct. The distinction between causes and grounds is central to the analysis of social action, but it is often blurred in everyday life and even in the social sciences. The efficient causes or antecedent conditions sought in empirical science are observable phenomena of the same type as the effects to be explained. For example, when Pareto explains opposition he correlates successful dissent with elite incapacity for effective violence and/or effective manipulation. (1) Similarly Gurr associates opposition with relative deprivation, the "perceived discrepency between men's value expectations and their value capabilities." (2) Both elite incapacity and relative deprivation are empirical conditions, not grounds or justifications. The facts of elite incapacity or relative deprivation become related to grounds only when they are compared to an ideal normative standard, which is not an impirical phenomenon. For example, if one believes that government should be strong enough to enforce its directives, elite incapacity would be a ground for opposition, as it was for Hobbes. That Hobbes also believed that elite incapacity was a condition for opposition does not destroy the distinction between cause and ground. Similarly, if one believes that one's value expectations should be realized, then relative deprivation would be a ground for opposition. Grounds, then, are associated with "ought" statements while causes are associated with "is" statements.

The confusion between grounds and causes in ordinary discourse and in social science arises most frequently from interpreting grounds as causes. Brinton, for example, in his discussion of revolutions, states that "men may revolt partly or even mainly because they are hindered," but that "also to themselves - they must appear wronged": (3) "'Cramp' must undergo moral transfiguration before men will revolt." (4)   In the terms of the present discussion, "moral transfiguration" means giving grounds for opposition by reference to an ideal. The ideal itself, however, is not a cause, although commitment to the ideal or the desire to realize it may function as causes. It may even be a necessary condition for oppositions that grounds be given for them, that at least some participants are committed to grounds, or that grounds be used as rationalizations for interests. Regardless of how grounds become motivated, however, they make the phenomenon of opposition public and intelligible by offering putative justification for it.   Every social organization has a normative or ideal dimension in terms of which its performance may be judged. Often there are competing or complementary sets of criteria by which performance may be judged. Criticism in terms of such ideal criteria takes the form of offering grounds.

The distinction between grounds and causes is rooted in Kant's distinction between practical anthropology and ethics. For Kant, practical anthropology was the study of the causes of human conduct, the laws of inclination or interest, while ethics was the study of the principles by which conduct is justified. (5)   Kant believed that the ideal of right conduct had to be motivated by a good will to be effective, but that it made such good will intelligible by defining its form. The present discussion does not depend upon a single ethical ideal, but follows Kant by differentiating the ideal from the empirical dimension of conduct. Were grounds irrelevant to oppositions, then oppositions would merely be clashes of interest. The use of grounds, even if only as rationalizations for interest, give oppositions an ideal dimension. Whether commitment to grounds is in good faith or not is an empirical question, the answer to which will vary in different cases.   The ideal dimension, however, gives oppositions their public meaning and purpose.

The analysis of the grounds for bureaucratic opposition has both psychological and social dimensions. Although most of the motives for opposition are grounded in the organization's structure or in wider social norms there is a category of motives which are purely personal and subjective, or "ungrounded." For example, members of an opposition may be motivated by idiosyncratic whim ("my boss has a certain je ne sais quoi which makes me hate him and want to do him in"), personal ambition ("if this policy can be changed I will have a better chance of being promoted"), and psychiatric malaise (the person is just disruptive for one reason or another). The presence of subjective motives for oppositional activity is used by administrators to brand all such activity as arbitrary, pathological, irrelevant, and ill-advised. Hence, in any extended oppositions such motives must be concealed and publicly replaced by references to grounded abuses. Those with subjective motives for opposition, then, usually join or recruit others who are committed to more "noble" aims.

Although the evidence is not as complete as one might wish, it appears that at least one member of any bureaucratic opposition is impelled by ungrounded motives, which may or may not be supplemented by concern to eliminate perceived abuses.

An example of the interplay between grounds and motives in an opposition is reported by a minor executive at a small but very successful manufacturing firm which was incorporated into a large conglomerate. (6) According to this executive, an incompetent superior, who was afraid to make any decisions, stymied the effectiveness of the small group under his authority. Although all of the four subordinates were frustrated, my informant indicated that he did not think that any action would have been taken had it not been for the overweening ambition of one member of the group. In this case, the efficient cause for the opposition was ambition while the ground was deviation from the ideal of efficiency. In other oppositions the efficient cause can be commitment to an ideal.

The grounds for oppositions are relative to the ideals brought to bear on concrete situations. Many bureaucratic oppositions are grounded in resistance to violations of purely bureaucratic norms, such as those defined by Max Weber in his ideal-typical bureaucracy. (7) Such conditions as injustice, dishonor, and incompetence are infractions of administrative rules and provide justification for opposition. Similarly, inefficient or ineffective policies violate the principle of instrumental rationality, the "regulative idea" of administration. However, bureaucratic oppositions may also be grounded in wider moral norms such as fairness or some such ultimate ethical principle as the categorical imperative to treat others as ends, never as means only. Despite the various criteria, however, all grounds have in common their appeal to ideal standards and their aim at justification.

ABUSES GROUNDED IN DEVIATIONS FROM
THE BUREAUCRATIC IDEAL

Abuses related to deviations from the administrative ideal involve issues of justice, efficiency, or honor. In Weber's discussion of the bureaucracy, workers are interpreted as mere functionaries who perform only their prescribed tasks and who treat every problem in accordance with the written rules, which refer to the proper handling of cases, not of people. One is to conduct one's office "without regard for person." Rules, rather than passions, are supposed to govern the bureaucrat's activities. Of course, rule compliance has just as much of an emotional basis as has rule violation, if the impact of habit is eliminated. According to the bureaucratic ideal, however, only those emotions which support rule compliance are admitted. Failure to perform according to the rules, either because of total disregard for them (arbitrary despotism) or because of subjective considerations such as racial prejudice, greed, or sexual attraction, constitutes bureaucratic malfeasance. Malfeasance is defined here as the inconsistent application or disregard of "the rules." The charge of malfeasance as a ground for bureaucratic opposition implies that all parties agree on the way in which the rule should be applied. When there is disagreement on the interpretation of the rules (which rules should apply to given cases and what a rule means) the grounds for opposition concern policy differences and not malfeasance. Although the distinction between policy differences and malfeasance is conceptually clear, the lines are blurred in practice because accused malfeasants often claim that oppositions against them are based on substantive disputes.

Charges of malfeasance can focus on the formal equality of rule application or on substantive effects of rule violation. Justice within organizations refers to the consistent, fair, and universalistic application of the rules. Injustice can be directed against subordinates or against relevant publics. In the latter instance, the groups, such as taxpayers, welfare recipients, or customers, may organize in opposition to the organization, but such activity is not a bureaucratic opposition. Subordinates who witness or experience injustice or unfairness often feel a sense of moral outrage, particularly if they have little authority. A worker in the cost accounting department of a large industrial corporation communicates such outrage in less than impeccable grammar:

My climatic opposition with Mr. V began when Gloria and I implored him to show us where it is a written policy of the company that allows him to deviate so far from the normal practices of the company. We wanted to know how he was personally permitted to set double standards (where only the male accountants could go on paid trips to various plants) for his employees, when he knew some of the rules he enforced were based on convention. N.C.'s corporate office has a reputation of being very liberal in regards to its employees as far as benefits, promotions, etc. for both sexes. That is why it was so difficult to accept or conform to the stringent rules of this one maniac. (8)

In another case, the supervisor of the research staff in a production department regularly issued "discriminatory task assignments." A bureaucratic opposition began when

> ... only those members of the Staff who felt that they had been discriminated against because of race or sex, took the initiative to meet with the Office Manager (supervisor's superior) ... The complaints were never investigated and the Office Manager reported the visits to the Supervisor. ... In an effort to discourage and prevent future contacts, he scrutinized the work of these employees who visited the Office Manager. When mistakes were found, no matter how insignificant, the employees were told that they were fired. (9)

In both these instances the bureaucratic opposition did not meet with initial success. The eventual achievement of their goals, the removal of the malfeasants, was secured by informing higher administrators of the dysfunctional consequences of norm violation. Administrators' awareness of the violations themselves was not sufficient to secure remedial action. These cases are indicative of a general pattern in which injustice, in itself, is insufficient to cause removal.

Fortunately, from the viewpoint of oppositionists, injustice, including the use of arbitrary power, rarely fails to violate the norms of efficiency and/or honor. Further, many instances of injustice also fall under the category of corruption, and thus are viewed by higher authorities as serious infractions, so long as these authorities are not themselves involved in the corrupt practices. David H. Bayley, a political scientist, states that corruption, "while being tied particularly to the act of bribery, is a general term covering misuse of authority as a result of considerations of personal gain, which need not be monetary." (10) This definition can encompass activities within both public agencies and "private" profit-making corporations. Yet the literature on corruption has been confined for the most part to the polity and its organizations. (11) This lopsided emphasis on corruption in the public sector is due, perhaps, to the widespread idea that business organizations are subject to the discipline of the marketplace and will simply go bankrupt at no one's loss but their own if they are too corrupt. Government, on the other hand, is supported by the taxpayer's money and, according to the conventional wisdom, has no institutional check on its inefficiency. Business corruption, then, is widely interpreted as being harmful only to the business, while governmental corruption is interpreted as being harmful to the public. In an economy ruled by oligopolies which are bailed out by government when they are on the verge of bankruptcy, the distinction between business and governmental corruption has little practical meaning. However, persistence of the myth of market discipline influences the relative importance of charges of corruption in different organizations and, therefore, the strategies pursued by bureaucratic opposition groups.

As implied in the definition, the motive for corruption is to obtain personal benefits beyond those stipulated in the contract of employment. One major characteristic of all modern bureaucracies is that an incumbent does not own his or her office. A salary is paid and perhaps other clearly specified perquisites are provided, but there is a prohibition on exchanging the power of one's office for additional benefits. In some organizations the separation of office from personal benefit is widely honored, while in others it is barely existent. The distinction between corruption committed by an isolated individual and corruption endemic to an organization is crucial for understanding bureaucratic oppositions. Confronting and attempting to remove or change the behavior of a lone malfeasant is quite different from being embedded in an organization in which corrupt activity is a common practice. Corrupt organizations often respond to opposition by trying to make it appear that infractions were not condoned and that isolated violators will be punished. In his efforts to clean up the New York City police force Serpico's initial failures were largely due to his naive judgment that the corruption was an individual and not an organizational phenomenon. When the truth finally got through to him, rather painfully, he changed his oppositional tactics. Of course, as will be indicated in subsequent chapters, the most appropriate tactics do not guarantee the success of a bureaucratic opposition.

When corruption is widespread within an organization it is often interpreted as normal behavior and scarcely perceived to be a norm violation. In speaking with numerous policemen in the service of a large midwestern city, only one complained, and did so bitterly, about the ubiquitous corruption. He was clearly pained by the disregard of his colleagues for "the rules." He himself accepted no bribes, either in goods or cash, from drug dealers trying to avoid arrest. He claimed that he knew of only one other officer with such scruples. His inability to act in ways that he thought proper led him finally to resign from the force. His crise de conscience aroused my interest. Why had none of the others complained? When I asked them how they handled corruption a pattern emerged. All of those to whom I spoke, with the exception of the officer discussed above, had relatives who were policemen. It was through them that they had learned what to expect. They were convinced, before personally confronting the corruption, that things were as they should or "had to" be and, thus, that there was no need to change them.

Another consideration with regard to bureaucratic opposition to corruption is who benefits when there is pervasive corruption. That is, when the rules are broken do the gains devolve directly to the individuals involved or does the organization as a whole stand to benefit from the practices? (12) When the primary beneficiary is the organization itself, the ground of opposition ought not to be classified as rule violation. Whether the instance is bribes paid to foreign officials by American multinational corporations, or surveillance of civilians by the military, or a company's keeping two sets of quality-control books to deceive health inspectors, such cases have more in common with disputes over policies and their implementation.

When incumbents of bureaucratic roles break the organization's rules, however, whether by applying the rules with partiality or by ignoring the rules altogether, their actions constitute formal breaches of justice. As noted, such infractions may and do, by themselves, constitute grounds for some bureaucratic oppositions. Structurally, rule infraction may be considered as an abuse or misuse of authority, while motivationally it is a spur to moral outrage over inequity, unfairness or dishonesty.

The consequences of deviations from organizational norms may, independently or in conjunction with injustice, constitute grounds for bureaucratic oppositions. Perhaps the most important possible effect of rule infraction is the reduction in or elimination of the organization's efficiency. One of the common justifications for bureaucracy is its supposed greater efficiency than preceding organizational forms. Efficiency refers to the effective achievement of the organizational goal, whatever it may be. Explicit division of labor, hierarchy of authority, conduct of office without regard for persons, and appointment and promotion of individuals to positions on the sole basis of their competency are defining characteristics of a bureaucracy, all of which are designed to augment efficiency. Specific sets of rules cover each of these general norms and when such rules are violated the organization is likely to become inefficient. Of course, inefficiency does not always result from rule infraction. For example, violation of the division of labor, as when colleagues in different departments give unauthorized aid to one another, may even make the organization more efficient, at least in the short run. However, despite the debate in the organizational literature over the effects of some of the bureaucratic norms on efficiency, there is general agreement that application of the norm of competence is essential for maximum efficiency.

In a literal and formal sense the superiors of an incompetent employee are the ones who have violated the norm of competence. However, bureaucratic oppositions directed against incompetence usually focus on the incompetent officials, not on those responsible for their appointment. Cases in which oppositions are aimed at those who made hiring and promotion decisions are usually grounded in charges of discrimination; that is, someone has not been hired or promoted because of prejudice against an ascriptive characteristic such as sex, age, race, or religion. The proliferation of national voluntary groups to counteract discrimination (for example, for blacks, women, and gays) has provided support to bureaucratic oppositions against discrimination. Such oppositions are usually fought on the grounds of injustice, although incompetence and, perhaps, dishonor may also be reasons.

The structural ground for an opposition against incompetence is that the role incumbent is not discharging assigned duties. Subordinates who must follow inappropriate orders are usually aware that their own performance is impaired. Thus, opposition to incompetence is often bound up with concern for career advancement, the desire to do meaningful and high-quality work, commitment to the norms of just rewards and equal opportunity, and concern for the deleterious effects of inappropriate or self-defeating action. The crew on Captain Arnheiter's Naval vessel judged their superior to be incapable of giving orders and mutinied. Mutiny is a special case of bureaucratic opposition because there is no higher authority to whom to appeal, it requires direct action, and, most importantly, it involves a usurpation of authority. Just as in the fictional "Caine Mutiny," the "Arnheiter Affair" led to a court-martial of the mutineers. In the latter case the court did not agree with the mutineers' assessment of their superior's competence.

Many issues are involved in understanding bureaucratic incompetence. Is it based on intellectual incapacity to perform role requirements or is it rooted in psychological factors? Are incompetent officials appointed because the norms have not been applied correctly or does incompetence only become manifest after the official has taken the position? Is there, perhaps, something about the structure of bureaucracies themselves or about positions of authority that fosters incompetence? Another set of issues relates to the perception of incompetence. Superiors often seem to suffer from what Josiah Royce called "viciously acquired naivete" about the excellence of their appointees or immediate subordinates. Is it merely that superiors do not want to admit to incorrect hiring and promotion procedures or to mistakes in applying good procedures? Or are subordinates more likely to perceive incompetent administration because they are directly involved in its effects? Although some people are fired or, more rarely, demoted, does a criterion such as "their attitude" play a greater part in their removal than does incompetence? In summary, if bureaucracies attempt to pursue goals efficiently, why are so many incompetents found in modern organizations?

One way of responding to the issues involved in bureaucratic incompetence is to investigate why incompetents are not removed. Most bureaucracies make little provision for dismissing employees and, as Weber noted, "Normally, the position of the official is held for life, at least in public bureaucracies; and this is increasingly the case for all similar structures." (13) In a discussion of public bureaucracies Blanche Blank remarks,

> If getting good people in has its frustrations, getting poor ones out is even worse. Dismissals in the New York City civil service run to less than 1.5 per cent a year. The required proceedings are highly formal, almost like a trial - and generally suggestive that it is the supervisor rather than the employee who is being tried. ... Considering, therefore, the risk of the unsettling effects on various segments of personnel, the tremendous consumption of agency time, the heavy cost and the ordinary human reluctance to do unpleasant things, it is remarkable that any dismissals are achieved under present conditions. (14)

Lawrence Peter (15) explains endemic incompetence in organizations by arguing that people are rewarded for doing their jobs well by promotion to other jobs which usually have more status, higher income, and greater power. Competent performance of a new task will eventuate in still another promotion. However, when an employee no longer performs adequately the promotion process will end. Over time, then, positions tend to be filled by incompetents. For example, excellent teachers may become bad principals, superb craftsmen may become grouchy and ineffective foremen, and hot-shot salespeople may become unproductive sales managers. Peter traces the problem of incompetence to the evaluation of candidates for a position on the basis of past performance at tasks that are not related to the functions of the new job. Hence, bureaucracies create incompetents.

Despite its great popularity among employees of large organizations, who assume that it applies to their bosses and not to themselves, "Peter's Principle" is a bit too glib to be accepted at face value. Why do many observations seem to support the "principle"? One possibility is that the new job differs in essential respects from the old one. One may perform a task well not only because one has been trained adequately for it but because it affords intrinsic value, regardless of its financial, status, and/or power rewards. People promoted to administrative positions are often judged to be incompetent. They have been removed from performing activities that they may have enjoyed and for which they were well suited, and they have been given the task of controlling others. Unless one enjoys exercising power over others or is satisfied fully by extrinsic financial and status gains, promotion into administration may be, at best, a mixed blessing. Perceived incompetence may stem not only from a deficiency in control skills and other administrative talents, but from resentment at being deprived of satisfying work. Administration is the "art" of getting others to do a task efficiently. Managers may miss the direct satisfaction of doing something concrete, be it making a sale, teaching a course, or handling a welfare client's problem. Since Marx's writings appeared, those concerned with worker alienation have considered control over one's work and its conditions to be the most important occupational value. They have failed to note, probably for ideological reasons, that form of alienation related to lack of direct control which is inherent in administrative roles.

In more general terms, of course, any or all aspects of a bureaucrat's job may be alienating. In the syndrome of alienation the person cannot identify with his or her work, therefore, the work loses its subjective meaning. The worker becomes less devoted and less efficient, and often tries to avoid making decisions. Marx's notion of alienation, although it was meant to apply to blue-collar work, is just as applicable, if not more so, to the jobs of white-collar bureaucrats:

> What do we mean by the alienation of labor? First, that the work he performs is extraneous to the worker, that is, it is not personal to him, is not part of his nature; therefore he does not fulfill himself in work, but actually denies himself; feels miserable rather than content, cannot freely develop his physical and mental powers, but instead becomes physically exhausted and mentally debased. Only while not working can the worker be himself; for while at work he experiences himself as a stranger. (16)

People who experience themselves as "other-than-themselves" are not only capable of inefficiency but of outright cruelty. Controls such as guilt and ideals of humaneness function in the autonomous person, not in those who are strangers to themselves.

From Here to Eternity (17) can be interpreted as the novelist James Jones's attempt to illustrate the tyranny and abuse leveled at subordinates by a compulsive and merciless individual who is alienated from his meaningless job. Less vicious, but perhaps more insidious, is the behavior of Bob Slocum, the anti-hero of Josepf Heller's Something Happened. (18) Employed as a middle-level administrator in a large and nameless business organization, Slocum is the epitome of the alienated bureaucrat. His treatment of his subordinates, colleagues, and family is often cruel and arbitrary. From his interior monologue we learn that he is as confused by his Kafkaesque actions as are those around him. (19)

The incompetence that results from resentment and alienation may have consequences beyond the inadequate performance of specialized tasks. It may also be the underlying reason for acts that form the basis of other grounds for bureaucratic opposition, such as injustice and dishonor. In the managerial ideology administration is the highest form of work and is judged to be universally desirable. Challenging this pervasive assumption reveals the possibility that the administrative myth is a subtle form of ressentiment and that hierarchical organization may have built-in psychological strains that engender inefficiency. (20).

In addition to the structural determinants of incompetence there are many psychological and social-psychological explanations for it. Some analysts of society have argued that the exercise of power itself has deleterious effects on those who employ it. When political scientists assess opposition to authoritarian regimes they often quote Lord Acton's dictum that "Power tends to corrupt: absolute power corrupts absolutely." (21) More to the point, perhaps, is a statement made by a black sheep of the American Revolution, Sam Adams: "Power is intoxicating. There have been few men who, when possessed of unrestrained power, have not made a very bad use of it." (22) Administrators do not, as a rule have absolute or unrestrained power. However, due to the difficulty of removing officials as noted above and other considerations to be discussed later, the supposed checks on managerial power, such as the observations of superiors and the performance of subordinates, are ineffective restraints.

A psychiatrist, Dr. H. Waldo Bird, identifies a set of personality characteristics which he claims are responsible both for propelling his male subjects to the top of organizations and for their incompetence and subsequent failure. In the successful men he observed, including those "whose corrupt behavior, sexual misadventures, incompetence or breakdowns have made news headlines recently, ... (the) drive for authority, control, and domination assumes overwhelming proportions as does the sex drive ...." (23) Other observers identify what may be called "male menopause" or "mid-life crisis" as a cause of incompetence. A journalistic account of such a crisis cites the example of "a 37-year-old production manager (who) began dumping all his office responsibilities on subordinates, some of them untrained to handle them, and filling his own day with unimportant work." (24) The so-called male menopause is not, according to the proponents of this explanation, a physiological phenomenon, but the result of highly career-conscious people recognizing that they are not going to "make it to the top" or that the position they had struggled for and finally achieved is not rewarding after all.

In attempting to account for incompetence one should not overlook the effects of alcoholism and the various types of mental illness which are widespread in the public at large. The Catholic Church and some unions and corporations have acknowledged the frequent incidence of alcoholism and have begun clinics for those who voluntarily undergo treatment or who are persuaded to do so. The medical profession classifies alcoholism and mental disorders as illnesses, attempting to remove the stigma of personal responsibility from them. However, many individuals are reluctant to admit, either to others or to themselves, that they suffer from such afflictions. Some bureaucratic oppositions are, of course, struggles against administrators who are mentally ill or alcoholics. Even if the oppositionist is sympathetic to the superior's plight such benevolent emotions must be overcome by an attitude of ruthless compassion which focuses upon objectionable actions. A male nurse who participated in a bureaucratic opposition to remove the Director of Nursing Services at a suburban community hospital at which he was employed reported,

> Most significant was the inflexibility of the Director, partially based on false information given her, and her own personal problems which clouded her judgment. She was rumored to drink heavily to the point that she was home 'ill' many times and when at work acted 'peculiar' and used mouth deodorants excessively. (25)

Inflexibility, such as that exemplified by the Director of Nursing Services, constitutes the basis of a number of related theories of organizational incompetence. Victor Thompson coined the term "bureaupathology" to identify the various manifestations of inflexibility, which run the gamut from personal problems to what Thorstein Veblen called "trained incapacity" (overspecialization). (26) Overspecialized bureaucrats cannot adapt to changes within the organization or the society at large and, thus, evince incompetence. For example, the introduction of computer technology or the rise of the black liberation movement probably caused many administrators to become incompetent because they were not flexible enough to cope with and adapt to new demands and requirements.

Robert K. Merton has investigated the structural factors that lead to the formation of the inflexible "bureaucratic personality." Merton asserts that conformity to the rules, the reliability of behavior, is essential to an efficient bureaucracy. Such conformity can best be achieved "if the ideal patterns are buttressed by strong sentiments which entail devotion to one's duties, a keen sense of the limitations of one's authority and competence, and methodical performance of routine activities." (27) Often such sentiments are overstressed in order to insure compliance and there occurs a "transference of the sentiments from the aims of the organizaiton onto the particular details of behavior required by the rules. Adherence to the rules, originally conceived as a means, becomes transformed into an end-in-itself." (28) Thus, Merton suggests that inflexible, and therefore potentially incompetent people, are trained to be so by the bureaucracy itself. Others have suggested that the inflexible bureaucrat manifests a particular personality type which was nurtured and developed in early childhood (for example, the "anal-retentive" personality). The presence of such people in organizations would be attributed to self-selection.

That rigid adherence to rules is often incompetent behavior which affects the organization adversely shows that the rules do not always promote efficiency and that incompetence can result from following them. This judgment is illustrated by the well-known protest tactic of "work-by-rule." Traffic controllers at airports have effectively stopped all plane traffic by this procedure and it is sometimes one of the tactics of bureaucratic opposition.

The inflexibility of a superior becomes a barrier to efficiency when there is a breach between the formal rules of an organization and the informal, everyday procedures that often grow up in efforts to adapt the rules to concrete situations. (29) An FBI agent considered the excessive phone calls and the "insipid and insistent suggestions" of his headquarters supervisor to be an attempt at "trying to look competent rather than be competent." (30) When the agent was disciplined for failing to write up a report on a tip provided by an informant who was known for his unreliability, his colleagues supported him in a bureaucratic opposition. They demonstrated to the higher echelon that the supervisor's over-rigid adherence to details constituted interference with the agency's mission and that the agent had been unfairly punished.

Inflexible adherence to rules may be due neither to personality nor to bureaucratic training, but may result from a feeling of "having" to prove to others that one is competent. Such overcompensation is especially prevalent among those whose ascriptive characteristics differ from the qualities of the "normal" role incumbent (for example, women, non-whites, and the very young).

The first female supervisor at a nationwide shipping company, N. was put in charge of a highly effective loading dock. According to one of her subordinates, high morale had resulted in a system of mutual aid which was at variance with the rules. N. recognized the efficiency of this informal system and felt at ease with it until she attended a meeting with other supervisors and managers. One can only speculate about what went on at the meeting, but when N. returned she "began to raise hell. She said that we (the workers) didn't run the area and she did." (31) Exercising her authority, she permitted no talking on the job, transferred workers to different positions arbitrarily, and prohibited the mutual assistance activities. The group's efficiency dropped precipitously and then decreased still further as the workers retaliated in a greve du zele. N. eventually quit. Because N. was a female in a previously all-male position, she was judged by special standards; her peers and superiors were concerned with her style, not with her achievement. A male, especially a white middle-aged male, would probably not have been singled out as being too easy. Due to the pressures on women to overstress the masculine stereotype of management it is a wonder that many more are not strict and "bitchy."

Rigid rule enforcement becomes incompetence in several ways. In addition to the possibility that the rules themselves generate inefficiency, subordinates may, like Dostoevsky's underground man, resist being "piano keys" or being treated as machines which are turned on at a specific hour, programmed to perform certain motions, and then turned off at another specific time. Informal systems may grow up as a response to the mechanization of the individual and may indicate an assertion of individual will. The desire to exert one's will for its own sake (Dostoevsky's "freedom to be free") sabotages many administrative plans to increase efficiency by changing the rules. The hope that "rational" changes will increase compliance is frequently dashed by the creation of ever-new informal networks. Administrators tend to rationalize their failures by accusing their employees of laziness or irresponsibility, because their perspective does not allow them to acknowledge mere willfulness. A common example of such administrative tunnel vision involves time regulations. Employees may take 40 minutes for lunch when the rules allow them only half an hour. The "enlightened" manager, who does not want to punish but who does want to maintain control, revises the rules to read "40 minutes for lunch." Shortly afterwards the employees begin to take 45 or 50 minutes for their mid-day meal. Rigid rule enforcement, then, is often perceived as an attack on one's dignity, a denial of one's volition. A common response to the perceived denial of dignity is to assert one's will, which within organizations usually can only be done by rule violation. If the rules are so engineered that they produce efficiency when they are obeyed, the assertion of will as a reaction to rigid enforcement leads to a reduction of organizational efficiency.

In addition to the various structural, psychological, and social-psychological explanations of incompetence, there is another determinant which might be termed rational or purposive. In this case people do not perform their role requirements competently because they find that the requirements are not in their own best interest. Most instances of incompetence grounded in rational self-interest are classified under corruption, but one may imagine examples in which people are purposefully inefficient so that they can hold on to jobs that would disappear if they were done effectively. For example, corruption, whether it is interpreted as injustice or incompetence or both by those who oppose it, has consequences for the character of opposition. In publicly exposing the considerable cost overruns of the C5A cargo jet project, Ernie Fitzgerald stressed the resultant inefficiency rather than the possible kick-backs, post-retirement job offers, etc., that led officials of the Defense Department to award and oversee contracts so ineffectively. A study of the former Air Force engineer's case suggests that, whatever the motive for Fitzgerald's "whistle-blowing" bureaucratic opposition, he believed that an appeal to the ground of incompetence rather than to that of injustice would be more prudent. (32)

In addition to incompetence, a second possible effect of norm violation is the denial of respect or of honor to other persons, whether subordinate employees or members of the organization's clientele. As a ground for opposition, disrespect is specifically the subjection of persons to demands that are beyond their role requirements. These requirements are defined by the organization's rules, although they tend to be less explicit for clients than for employees. For example, a chairperson may require that faculty attend departmental meetings, meet their assigned classes, and turn in grades on time. These demands are within the chairperson's rights, because they match the explicit duties of each faculty member. However, a chairperson who uses departmental funds to purchase equipment for private use, indulgently forces secretaries to witness abusive temper tantrums, or insists that faculty host departmental social events at their own expense abuses authority and violates the rules. Such actions as displays of temper and extra demands on employees are not only instances of injustice, but of dishonor. They require subordinates to act in ways that are undefined by, if not irrelevant to, their role descriptions.

A Chicago legal secretary was fired because she refused, even after receiving a written directive, to make coffee for the lawyers for whom she worked. With the aid of other secretaries in the office, who came to work in waitress' uniforms to protest her dismissal, and the news media, a successful bureaucratic opposition of two week's duration resulted in her reinstatement. Since the expectation that secretaries make coffee for their superiors is general in organizations one might inquire why there have not been many more of such oppositions. Only recently have secretaries begun to define their role as excluding the "traditional" functions of women, a change associated with the Women's Liberation Movement. Under the new definition, only strictly secretarial tasks, such as taking dictation and typing, are perceived to be legitimate demands, while the performance of "wifely" or "motherly" functions is interpreted as degrading. That the performance of duties extrinsic to the secretarial role is not yet widely perceived to be dishonorable, and may even be regarded as an honor, is related to the lack of self-respect of many women. Without self-respect the experience of dishonorable treatment is impossible.

One source of dishonor, then, is the merging of ascriptive characteristics and the behavioral expectations based on them with occupational role expectations. The more that a single ascriptive group dominates an occupation or clientele, the more likely it is that there will be dishonorable treatment. The cultural ground of violation of the bureaucratic norm of treatment "without regard for person" is often supplemented, or supplanted, by idiosyncratic prejudice. An assistant to a bank branch manager in the Southeast was infuriated by her superior's disrespect for her. He called her one of the "girls," frequently asked her to bring him coffee, and made cracks about "libbers." Believing that virtue would triumph, that her superiors would acknowledge her excellence and punish the incompetence of her immediate boss, she refused to object to the degrading treatment. (33)

Social movement organizations, such as the National Organization for Women, the Grey Panthers, the NAACP, and gay rights groups, attempt to combat dishonor and disrespect. One of their basic tactics is consciousness raising, which is intended to give their constituents a sense of pride in themselves. Such pride, however, has the effect of making people more aware of and vulnerable to the experience of dishonor. These movement organizations have lobbied for laws and enforcement mechanisms to end dishonorable treatment, but for political reasons they have often phrased their objectives exclusively in terms of justice. The results of their efforts, such as the creation of the Equal Employment Opportunity Commission, have aided some bureaucratic oppositions. The rights movements also attempt to educate the public, which includes organizational authorities, about the invalidity and inhumane consequences of the stereotyping which is the basis of much disrespective treatment.

Violation of rules specifying the rights of employees or clients can be opposed on the grounds of both injustice and disrespect. However, the motivational ground for members of a bureaucratic opposition is usually dishonor. When the clients are dishonored, bureaucratic oppositions in their favor usually occur when they are in a relatively weak position with regard to the organization and have few resources to mount a defense on their own behalf. Action in behalf of clients is also more likely where the employees are professionals or semi-professionals whose occupational ideology stresses service to others. An example of concern for clients' rights (and of the preconditions for a bureaucratic opposition) is the following letter to an "action" column of a daily newspaper:

> We've seen the movie "One Flew Over the Cuckoo's Nest"; now what do we do about it? Both of us have been working in a private mental hospital ward in Chicago and have seen gross abuses in the use of electroshock here, and we want to know what we can do about it. Patients or their guardians are supposed to sign consent forms, but the formality is abused. Others sign for them or they simply are told to sign. We ... see no benefits and only pain from this often vindictive treatment. (34)

This letter also illustrates another feature of the grounds for bureaucratic opposition. The focus of the opposition may be on the rule violations themselves, whether formal (injustice) or substantive (incompetence or dishonor). However, the concern may also be with the violation of universal moral principles: the human consequences of rule violations. Victimization or empathy with it are frequent grounds for participating in a bureaucratic opposition. The indignity of dishonor, the frustration resulting from being subordinate to an incompetent, and the unwilling involvement in cruelty are all denials of a person's autonomy and provide much of the moral stimulus for risk taking. However, it is necessary to reiterate that there are usually multiple grounds for any bureaucratic opposition.

The preceding discussion has been an attempt to analyze a fundamental ground for bureaucratic opposition: organizational abuse resulting from norm violations. The following section will examine the second basic ground for opposition: abuses reflecting differences in values and in the interpretation of the policies intended to achieve goals. The major concern of the analysis of norm violation was to define the relevant norms and to illustrate briefly some of the consequences of their infraction. The issue of why the rules of bureaucracy are broken has not been considered extensively, because the focus has been on principles, not proclivities.

An adequate analysis of the reasons for norm infraction would require a typology distinguishing organizational from personal causes of rule violation. Among the organizational influences would be sets of contradictory expectations (for example, the strain between tenure and competency in academic institutions) which have been studied by organizational researchers. With regard to personal influences on rule infraction, there are three major classes. The first is the classical Greek understanding that norm violation is the result of some diminished intellectual capacity. The second is the Christian category of sin. The seven cardinal sins - avarice, lust, envy, wrath, pride, sloth, and gluttony - account for much of the behavior that we wish to understand. Finally, disobedience may be principled and purposive, an act of protest or opposition against the organization on moral grounds.

ABUSES GROUNDED IN DISPUTES OVER POLICIES

The majority of bureaucratic oppositions appear to be grounded in one or more violations of the norms that constitute the bureaucratic ideal. The abuses classed under the heading of norm infraction include such conditions as injustice, incompetence, and dishonor, each of which presupposes that all participants in the situation share a normative consensus but, for one reason or another, one or more individuals misbehave or deviate. In the society at large analogous behavior would be labeled criminal, immoral, or abnormal, and would be controlled by such methods as incarceration, psychotherapy, or ostracism. Those who have the authority to punish rule violators often fail to do so, both in the organization and society. A later chapter of this study will examine some of the reasons for the failure of administrators to mete out negative sanctions, but for the present it is sufficient to note that many bureaucratic oppositions stem from such inaction.

There are other grounds than norm infraction on which bureaucratic oppositions are based. These grounds can be grouped together under the heading of disputes over organizational policy and focus on abusive rules rather than abusive persons. Of course, the distinction between rules and persons is relative, because particular individuals are often so closely associated with a policy that an opposition may aim at their removal in conjunction with policy changes. In addition, oppositionists may believe that some rule violations are rooted in policies that are vague, inapplicable, inappropriate, or otherwise problematic.

Policies may be judged to be objectionable because they contradict general bureaucratic norms or because they are inconsistent with the particular goals that differentiate the organization from others. In such cases the standards for criticism are embedded within the organization's self-definition. However, policies may also be opposed because they are held to violate general moral standards, such as those of a religious tradition, the general culture, or some transcendent position. As in the case of norm violations, policies may be disputed because they harm subordinate employees in some way or because they harm the organization's relevant public.

Table 2.1   Grounds of Bureaucratic Opposition, Organizational Abuses

	Rule Violations	Policy Disputes	
	Bureaucratic Norms		Moral Norms
Internal	Injustice (toward subordinates) Dishonor (of subordinates) Incompetency	Inefficient policies	Unfair policies

External	Injustice (toward relevant
	    publics and individuals)
	Dishonor (toward relevant
	    publics and individuals)
	Ineffective action
		Ineffective
		policies
			Immoral
			policies

The formal structure of opposition, noted by Georg Simmel among others, requires that there be some points of agreement among the conflicting parties in addition to the issues on which they disagree. When the opposition to an organization is grounded in policy disputes, the areas of agreement among the contenders are usually quite broad. In a sense, the opposition group is hoisting the organization by its own petard; the grievance is organizational hypocrisy. The oppositionists claim that the organization is not living up to its own standards or that its policies and their implementation are not adequate to achieve its stated goals. Martin Luther's objections to the selling of indulgences by the Catholic Church was, initially, nothing more than a bureaucratic opposition grounded in a dispute over policy. Luther's dissenting arguments were based on the New Testament, a book to which the Church claimed to adhere. According to Luther, the practice of selling indulgences was contrary to the Church's major purpose, the salvation of souls.

Disputes over policy may focus on internal issues of efficiency or external considerations of effectiveness. Efficiency, here, refers to the use of appropriate and economical means to achieve the organization's goals. Inefficiency is often more apparent to those who implement policies than to those who have the authority to make them or change them. This irony is a continual source of strain in organizations. Some organizations acknowledge the tension and encourage subordinates to suggest ways of increasing efficiency, even to the point of awarding cash bonuses for cost-reducing innovations. An Indiana-based pharmaceutical firm, for example, provides empolyees with one-third of the money saved each year by implementing their suggestions. In most cases, the administration and the subordinates should benefit from attempts to make policies more efficient. Thus, it is reasonable to assume that when bureaucratic oppositions coalesce around policy disputes something more than efficiency is at stake.

Behind some policy disputes concerning efficiency is opposition to an incompetent administrator, one who is inflexibly committed to tradition, a personal ideology, or a literal interpretation of the rules. Such disputes may also mask resistance to dishonor as the following example illustrates. In response to pilferage from its warehouse a large retail chain instituted a security policy in which drivers were ordered to unload their trucks and reload them while the invoice was checked against the goods. Although employees did not criticize the need for a security check they felt that this particular policy unduly harrassed them, forced them to do an excessive amount of work, and left them less time for the day's deliveries. Only the last complaint related to efficiency; the others were concerned primarily with dishonor. After complaining to the foreman without success, the workers attempted to have their union intercede for them. The steward, who was aware of the problem, indicated that the union approved of the company's policy. One driver interpreted the union's inaction in the following terms: "Deep down, the union felt that with their refusal to help, the employees would forget the whole matter and let the company do what they want." (35) The resulting bureaucratic opposition, which was initiated by those involved in the thefts, escalated into a work stoppage. After a week of protest the opposition was successful and the policy was changed to require only that the goods be checked against the invoice while they were being loaded onto the truck for the first time.

In contrast to inefficient policies, ineffective policies are those which in some way are deemed inconsistent with the organization's goals, for example, by subverting them or being irrelevant to them. A great many of the bureaucratic oppositions that have received public attention are grounded in ineffective policies - they have been attempts to redirect the organization towards its "proper" goal. "Sore Throat," a bureaucratic opposition composed of one or more employees of the American Medical Association, has exposed various policies that it considers inconsistent with the goals of the Association. For example, it publicized a policy which permits drug company representatives to sit on the scientific policymaking body of the Association because that policy contradicts the AMA's public claim to independence from the profitable pharmaceutical industry. (36) Other Sore Throat disclosures were aimed at demonstrating to the Internal Revenue Service that the AMA should be taxed on advertising revenues from its publications. Documents indicated AMA political contributions were aimed at preventing tax-reform legislation that would impose levies on advertising revenue. Sore Throat's objective was not merely to expose the financial interests and political lobbying of the AMA but to restore moral purpose to the Association: "Once in a financial shamble with its executives discredited, Sore Throat believes the AMA could 'be restored to its original constitutional objectives: To promote the science and art of medicine and the betterment of public health'." (37)

Oppositions grounded in resistance to ineffective policies confront the problem of identifying just what the organization's goals are. Organization theorists are notoriously divided over the proper way to determine goals, and even over the issue of whether they can be determined at all. Functionalists, such as Talcott Parsons and Peter Blau, identify goals on the basis of prior theoretical categories. If this approach is rejected in favor of an empirical analysis, the problem of finding a starting point arises. James D. Thompson argues that goals vary over time. Herbert Simon states that the goals "must be inferred from observation of the organization's decision-making processes," (38) and thus recognizes that there may be several, possibly conflicting, goals. Charles Warriner explicitly rejects determination based on official statements of purpose: they are "fictions produced by an organization to account for, explain, or rationalize its existence to particular audiences rather than ... valid and reliable indicators of purpose." (39) Yet for many people, including the members of bureaucratic oppositions, it is just such official statements that are believed to indicate the organization's goals. And it is to the goals mentioned in such pronouncements that they want to hold the organization accountable.

While some policies are in clear contradiction to the official goals of the organization, others are in a much more ambiguous relation. Is it a goal or a subgoal of the Federal Bureau of Investigation to obtain information about the intimate lives of public figures, such as Martin Luther King, Jr.? Was this policy of the FBI merely a reflection of J. Edgar Hoover's idiosyncracies or was it directly related to the organization's official and assigned mission? Such uncertainty and ambiguity have caused some bureaucratic oppositions to become mired in debates about the "true" goals of the organization and the fitness of policies to these goals.

A second and more serious problem confronted by oppositions to ineffective policies is the presence of two clearly distinct, and at times contradictory, sets of goals in all organizations. The first set contains the commonly understood aims of the organization, the products or services that it is supposed to provide. The second set comprises those goals related to the sheer continuation of the organization itself. Friedrich Baerwald refers to the first set of goals as the "object orientation" of a group and to the second as its "project orientation." (40) This distinction is similar to others, such as Edward Gross' differentiation of "output goals" from "support goals." (41) The object and project orientations of an organization are not necessarily contradictory, but in practice they often clash. For example, there have been allegations that the FBI had policies to foster rather than limit criminal activities. The aim of such policies, which are contradictory to the Bureau's object orientation, was to obtain additional Congressional funding (project orientation). As an example of this policy, a "paid snitch for the FBI," confessing to Otis Pike and his Congressional Committee on Intelligence, related "how the FBI paid him to lead a bunch of idealist ding-a-lings on a draft board raid: 'I was not only encouraging the group to raid the Camden draft board, I was initiating all the plans to do so'." (42)

Another case of conflict between object and project orientations concerns the conditions in a Chicago psychiatric hospital that led to a bureaucratic opposition. The opposition charged that the administration was primarily interested in maintaining the number of patients and in keeping the costs of their care to a minimum. The oppositionists, who saw the patients on a day-to-day basis and were members of the various "helping" professions, sought policies which would increase the quality of care. Prevailing policies were judged to be ineffective because the dissenters were committed to the facility's object orientation. (43)

In nonprofit organizations, financial interests form part of the project orientation. Businesses, however, present a special problem because there is disagreement about whether profits or the production of quality goods is the organization's primary object. Some social philosophers, such as Thornstein Veblen, have distinguished between "business" and "industry," identifying the first with the quest for profits and the second with quality production. They have adapted, then, the distinction between object and project orientations to the special case of capitalist economic organizations. Whatever the other problems with this distinction may be, it is useful for understanding bureaucratic oppositions in economic organizations. For example, when the Good Humor Corporation produced ice cream with dangerously high bacterial counts it did so in order to increase profits. It would have been costlier and less profitable to produce good ice cream, which their own advertising calls "the next best thing to love." Good Humor's pursuit of profit at the expense of quality and public health provoked a "whistle-blowing" opposition which was reported in the press. (44)

Project orientation, which refers to the perpetuation of the organization, often becomes confused with the continued domination of the organization's elite. Labor unions, despite their nominal democracy, are particularly subject to the replacement of the union's interests as a whole by the oligarchy's advantage.   Jock Yablonski's fate (he and his family were murdered) is testimony to the violence that often attends efforts to change formally democratic but effectively authoritarian organizations.   It does not follow, simply because the "machinery" of democracy is present, that those in power will allow it to be used. Roberto Michels' work is basic to understanding the reasons for oligarchic structures in formally democratic regimes, though his pessimism obscured recognition of such possibilities as oppositional movements.

Dissident groups within the Teamsters Union provide an example of opposition to an authoritarian union.   One such group, PROD, with two thousand members, reaches perhaps the upper limit in size for a bureaucratic opposition group.   PROD is primarily opposed to ineffective policies, although it has also attacked corruption and rule violation.   Its basic grievance is oligarchic domination enforced through policies which provide "its top brass with a fleet of luxurious jet aircraft," give them incomes of over $120,000 per year, and treat them to unlimited travel accounts and French chefs. (45) A second grievance, which also illustrates a concern for object orientation, is the charge that the union has not tried to achieve contracts which contain adequate safety clauses.   The assumption of the opposition, which is consistent with the cultural ideal of a labor union and the union's own charter, is that the goal of union includes on-the-job protection of its members. Bureaucratic oppositions in many other unions, such as the United Mine Workers, the National Maritime Union, and the International Ladies Garment Workers Union, have also been initiated on the grounds of ineffectiveness and corruption. (46)

Policies that are considered to be abusive because they are ineffective are sometimes indistinguishable from those which are judged unfair. Fairness is a moral standard which applies to relations within the organization, but which does not necessarily coincide with bureaucratic norms.   Fairness does coincide with those bureaucratic norms which prescribe equal treatment "without regard to persons" and hiring and promotion on the basis only of competence.   Hence, oppositions against policies which explicitly discriminate against one group of employees, such as women or minority group members, focus on both moral and formal abuses. Discriminatory policies are often in effect for long periods before they are judged to be unfair. Perception of their unfairness is often spurred by social changes external to the organization, such as the effects of the various liberation movements. The message of such movements is that traditional differences in treatment have been based upon erroneous and immoral assumptions about the character and capabilities of the members of certain groups. Bureaucratic oppositions grounded in the struggle for fairness have relatively good chances for success. Not only do they often have at their disposal the resources of national groups and access to legal remedies, but their moral purpose stimulates zeal and solidarity which are often absent in responses to norm infractions. Further, the administrators are often less implacable, more ready to yield, because discriminatory policies may contradict their own moral standards and those of the society at large.

When discriminatory policies are aimed at relevant publics or client groups rather than at the employees of an organization, the abuse is interpreted as a breach of the organization's function and is usually judged to be more reprehensible than "unfair" internal treatment. The greater public outrage at the unfair treatment of clients is probably due to identification with the victims (one might have been or might in the future be a client), the cultural separation between "public" and "private" activity, and the notion that people are free to change jobs but often cannot avoid the encroachment of an organization upon their lives.

Other charges of unfairness and of abuses grounded in policies which harm those outside the organization stem from commitment to absolute moral principles rather than from issues of effectiveness or efficiency. Perhaps the most relevant moral principle here is the prescription to treat people as ends-in-themselves, never as means only, which was formulated by Immanuel Kant as the "categorical imperative." (47)   The categorical imperative is inconsistent with bureaucratic rationality, which considers employees as means to enable effective and efficient goal attainment: they are mere role incumbents. Often when the goal of the organization is "service," clients are regarded as means to profits or as excuses for further government funding. Customers of production organizations are similarly viewed as means to profits, as is evidenced by much advertising.

An extreme case of the treatment of people as means to an organizational end is provided by various governmental bureaucracies, such as intelligence agencies, for which the goal is a reified public good. For example, "shortly before King was to be awarded the Nobel Peace Prize, the FBI sent him and his wife an anonymous letter, along with a tape from one of the 'bugs' (recordings made with the approval of Attorney General Robert Kennedy of King's conversations), which King took to be a suggestion that he commit suicide or face public disgrace." (48) Other FBI vendettas against persons from all sectors of the political spectrum have come to light, indicating gross violation of the categorical imperative. (49) Summing up the proceedings at a Senate hearing on this agency, columnist Ellis Cose writes:

> ... the feeling by the FBI (was) that once someone had been labeled as subversive (usually Communist) or was thought to have close as-sociations with subversives, any means of destroying that individual was justified. (50)

Disclosures of "wrong doing" by intelligence agencies before congressional committees and the Rockefeller Commission, and statements to the press by "disgruntled" employees intent upon reformist bureaucratic opposition indi-cate that abuses were not "isolated incidents of zealous agents exceeding authority in the field, however frequently such may occur. Rather, the abuses were ongoing, bureaucratic programs, often continuing over de-cades ...." (51) The nature of intelligence organizations, including their cult of secrecy, insistence on loyalty, and occasional use of violence, make bureaucratic oppositions aimed against their "immoral" policies difficult to undertake. The best known oppositions against such policies were undertaken by former CIA agents Victor Marchetti and Philip Agee, who "blew the whistle" from a relatively safe distance. Such oppositions are borderline cases which merge into public opposition to bureaucracy from the outside. Agee's struggle is also atypical because it had a revolutionary intent: he "feels that the abolition of the CIA is the only viable solution." (52) That Marchetti and Agee resigned their positions and literally risked their lives indicates that the motivational ground for their opposition was immoral policies and not merely infractions of bureaucratic norms.   Although intelligence agencies are often publicly opposed for their illegal actions, moral outrage seems to impel and sustain the struggle.

There are several possible explanations for the occurrence of immoral policies. Sometimes there has been a change in society's moral standards that has not been accompanied by alteration in policy. For example, intelligence agencies conceived and instituted in wartime conditions carry their policies forward into peacetime activity. A second explanation affixes cause and blame on individuals who abuse their authority. Much of the blame for the exposed wrongdoing of governmental agencies in the 1970s, for example, has been placed, with strong conservative implications, on "sick" or "wicked" men such as Hoover and Richard Nixon. More structural explanations for immoral policies center on the dynamics of what was called "project orientation" above. The desire to perpetuate the organization and its elite often results in policies that sacrifice persons to the bureaucratic equivalent of raison d' etat. Project orientation is intensified when the organization is locked in competition with other bureaucracies or groups. Business policies such as "planned obsolescence" and President Nixon's use of the FBI and the IRS to harrass his "enemies" exemplify this dynamic.

The myth of bureaucracy - that it is purely an administrative entity devoid of politics - does not allow for the identification of any of the abuses discussed in this chapter. That such abuses exist and that people have struggled to eliminate them is evidence against the validity of managerial ideology. Political activity is ubiquitous and is not confined to the state, despite the protestations of some social scientists. Political processes have similarities across disparate contexts, thus the work of those who have examined oppositions in the state is useful for the analysis of similar phenomena within organizations.   However, for reasons stated at the beginning of this chapter, political scientists have not attended sufficiently to the grounds for such oppositions, concentrating instead on the overt activities involved in conflict. For a study of bureaucratic oppositions, investigation of their grounds is essential because different grounds lead to different strategies and outcomes. This chapter presented a typology of the grounds for opposition, showing their structural and motivational aspects and revealing their origin in the perception of abuse. Abuses were classified in terms of violations of bureaucratic norms, inefficient and ineffective policies, and immoral policies.

Grounds are the "good reasons" or bases for action. Generally, before any concerted action can occur, or the plans for it even be formulated, people must have reason to depart from routine. Awareness of the grounds for opposition is often the result of a social process and is usually the first stage in constituting an opposition group. Such awareness is not only important from the viewpoint of self-knowledge but also because it is a tactic in group formation and in later struggles. Having detailed the grounds for opposition, the next step is to investigate the processes and problems of initiating bureaucratic oppositions.

CHAPTER 2: NOTES

(1) S.E. Finer (ed.), Vilfredo Pareto: Sociological Writings, New York: Praeger, 1966, p. 134.

(2) Ted Robert Gurr, Why Men Rebel, Princeton: Princeton University Press, 1970, p. 13.

(3) Crane Brinton, The Anatomy of Revolution, New York: Vintage, 1957, p. 36.

(4) Ibid.

(5) Immanuel Kant, Fundamental Principles of the Metaphysics of Morals, Indianapolis: Bobbs-Merrill, 1949.

(6) Student paper P.X.D., 1976. (These papers are unpublished class assignments in which the students are given an understanding of what a bureaucratic opposition is and then are asked to describe one fully in which they, or someone they knew well, were involved. All students were employed at the time.)

(7) Max Weber, "Bureaucracy," in From Max Weber: Essays in Sociology, H.H. Gerth and C. Wright Mills (eds.), New York: Oxford University Press, 1946, pp. 196-244.

(9) Student paper L.W., 1976, p. 5.

(10) David H. Bayley, "The Effects of Corruption in a Developing Nation," Western Political Quarterly XIX, #4 (December, 1966), p. 721. In the same vein J.S. Nye states: "Corruption is behavior which deviates from the formal duties of a public role because of private-regarding (personal, close family, private clique) pecuniary or status gains; or violates rules against the exercise of certain types of private regarding influence." (J.S. Nye, "Corruption and Political Development: A Cost-Benefit Analysis," American Political Science Review LXI, #2 (June, 1967), p. 419.

(11) For example, all of the three dozen selections in a book on official deviance avoid mention of corrupt practices in capitalist enterprises: Jack D. Douglas and John M. Johnson (eds.), Official Deviance: Readings in Malfeasance, Misfeasance, and other forms of corruption, Philadelphia: Lippincott, 1977.

(12) And if the organization is the primary beneficiary, there may or may not be rewards for those employees responsible.

(13) Max Weber, op.cit., p. 202.

(14) Blanche D. Blank, "The Battle of Bureaucracy," The Nation 203 (December 12, 1966), p. 636.

(15) Laurence J. Peter and Raymond Hull, The Peter Principle, New York: William Morrow, 1969.

(16) Karl Marx, "Alienated Labor," pp. 93-105 in Eric Josephson and Mary Josephson (eds.), Man Alone: Alienation in Modern Society, New York: Dell, 1962, p. 97.

(17) James Jones, From Here to Eternity, New York: Scribner, 1951.

(18) Joseph Heller, Something Happened, New York: Ballantine, 1975.

(19) For an excellent analysis of Slocum the bureaucrat see: James M. Glass, "Reality and Organization: The Executive as Depth Personality Structure," Paper delivered at the Northeast Political Science meetings, Jug End, Massachusetts, November, 1976; and James M. Glass, "Consciousness and Organization: The Disintegration of Joseph K. and Bob Slocum," Administration and Society 7 , #3 (November, 1975), 366-83.

(20) The term ressentiment is derived from Nietzsche, and has been elaborated, without the anti-religious connotations, by Max Scheler. It may be defined as repressed resentment at the inability to achieve a value that is overtly expressed as detraction from that value and those who have achieved it. (Max Scheler, Ressentiment, New York: Schocken Books, 1961).

(21) Letter to Bishop Mandell Creighton in 1887.

(22) Samuel Adams, 1722-1803, source unknown.

(23) Lois Timnick, "Twisted Power-Sex Drive Leads VIP Downfall," Chicago Daily News (June 3, 1977), 2.

(24) John F. Lawrence, "The Mid-life Crisis: When Male-Menopause Joke Isn't Funny," Chicago Sun-Times (July 5, 1977), 45.

(25) Student paper D.B., 1977, p. 2.

(26) Victor A. Thompson, Modern Organization. New York: Knopf, 1961.

(27) Robert K. Merton, "Bureaucratic Structure and Personality," pp. 195-206 in Social Theory and Social Structure. New York: Free Press, 1957, p. 198.

(28) Ibid., p. 199.

(29) It is this attempt to change formal rules, to try to institute more reasonable, efficient rules, that is the aim of some bureaucratic oppositions. It is the ground that is referred to as disputes over policies within the sphere of bureaucratic norms.

(30) Student paper K.K., 1977, p. 13.

(31) Student paper S.A., 1976, p. 4.

(32) Ralph Nader, Peter J. Petkas and Kate Blackwell (eds.), Whistle Blowing: The Report on the Conference on Professional Responsibility. New York: Grossman Publishers, 1972, pp. 46-52.

(33) Niki Scott, "Belle Bides Time with Nasty Boss," Chicago Sun-Times, (May 1, 1977), p. 4.

(34) "Action Line," Chicago Tribune, (April 20, 1976), section 2, p. 1.

(35) Student paper D.D., 1976, p. 10.

(36) "'Sore Throat' Attacks," Time, (August 18, 1975), p. 54.

(37) James Pearre, "AMA Sweats Out Case of 'Sore Throat'" Chicago Tribune, (August 17, 1975), p. 10.

(38) Herbert A. Simon, "On the Concept of Organizational Goal," Administrative Science Quarterly 7, #1 (June, 1964), 20.

(39) Charles K. Warriner, "The Problems of Organizational Purpose," Sociological Quarterly 6, #2 (Spring, 1965), 141.

(40) Friedrich Baerwald, "Humanism and Social Ambivalence," Thought XLII, #167 (Winter, 1967), 554.

(41) Edward Gross, "The Definition of Organization Goals," British Journal of Sociology XX, #3 (September, 1969), 284.

(42) Nicholas von Hoffman, "Witness for the Betrayal," Chicago Tribune (November 25, 1975), section 2, p. 4.

(43) Student paper, M.P., 1976.

(44) "Ice Cream Gate," Time (August 18, 1975), 67.

(45) James Strong, "Teamster 'Ripoff' Charged: Dissidents Assail 'Sky High' Salaries Paid Union Officials," Chicago Tribune (May 28, 1967), 1.

(46) For some examples see Burton Hall (ed.), Autocracy and Insurgency in Organized Labor, New Brunswick: Transaction Press, 1972.

(47) The significant difference between the categorical imperative and the golden rule is that the latter assumes, and does not make explicit, that one would treat oneself decently. Kant was not so optimistic.

(48) David C. Martin, "Probes Reveal Frequent Abuse of Nation's Intelligence Agencies," Indianapolis Star (December 14, 1975), 20.

(49) See Morton H. Halperin et al., The Lawless Crimes of the U.S. Intelligence Agencies, New York: Penguin Books, 1976.

(50) Ellis Cose, "The Unlearnable Lesson," Chicago Sun-Times, (November 24, 1975), 23.

(51) Halperin, op. cit., p. 4.

(52) Doug Porter and Margaret Van Houten, "CIA as White-Collar Mafia: Marchetti Ungagged," Village Voice (June 16, 1975), 43.

3 The Conditions of Bureaucratic Opposition

> ... if someone took it upon himself to alter the disposition of
> things around him he ran the risk of losing his footing and falling to
> destruction.
>
> — Franz Kafka, The Trial

It is a fallacy born of optimism to believe a thing necessarily will be done, simply because it should be done. As President Carter has said, "The world isn't fair." Thus, we may reasonably assume that changes are not made in bureaucracies just because there are abuses of moral and/or bureaucratic norms. The grounds for oppositions are all the reasons why subordinates may and sometimes do challenge the administrative order, but they are counter-balanced by the conditions of organizational life, most of which are directed to the results of uninterrupted functioning. The phenomenon of bureaucratic opposition may usefully be conceived of as a process in which the forces for change continually struggle against those promoting stability. Even when an overt opposition emerges, it remains subject to dissolution by the very dynamics of hierarchical systems as they influence both personality and the relations that bind informal groups together. It is essential for a comprehensive understanding of bureaucratic opposition, then, to grasp why people find it difficult to attempt to make changes which would bring practice into line with standards, and also to understand which conditions are most favorable to the emergence of resistance.

The conditions promoting stability have been discussed by social theorists primarily under the heading of "the problem of order": How is a stable and functioning society possible for individuals whose interests may conflict? Hobbes' response to this question is that rational human beings subordinate all particular interests to their supreme self-interest in survival, and, thus, will obey an effective sovereign regardless of the content of the commands. Rational individuals, according to Hobbes, prefer to be controlled because their alternative is to live in a state of nature where, in a condition of the war of "every man against every man," there is "continual fear and danger of violent death; and the life of man, solitary, poor, nasty, brutish, and short." (1) Three centuries after Hobbes the problem of order continues to be a central concern of social thought. Talcott Parsons, in "Hobbes and the Problem of Order," claims that Hobbes "saw the problem with a clarity which has never been surpassed." (2) Parsons, however, does not ground order primarily in force and fear but in value consensus, which is developed during the individual's socialization and is reinforced by various institutions.

Hobbes, the utilitarian, and Parsons, who acknowledges normative control, together provide the twin bases of most theories of order: interest and duty. A dissenting tradition, which is generally opposed to authority, supplements mainstream speculation with other conditions promoting stability. In the early modern period, for example, Étienne de La Boétie was concerned with the problem of order. Unlike Hobbes, however, he did not ask why people obey but why they do not disobey. La Boétie assumed that the ruler's power is partly dependent on the acquiescence of the ruled, on their consent. He conceded that fear, submission "under constraint and force," functions to insure initial compliance. But he noted that after the institution of a state most people "obey without regret and perform willingly what their predecessors had done just because they had to." (3) La Boétie was concerned with understanding why people obey a tyrant willingly when they are in no immediate danger, and he added to the grounds of interest and duty those of habit, propaganda, and cooptation. The grounds provided by both the mainstream and dissenting traditions in modern social thought are sufficient as points of departure for understanding the relative imbalance between the ubiquity of organizational abuses and the less common response of bureaucratic opposition.

The case data on bureaucratic opposition, which is used in other parts of this work, is not well adapted to the present issue. Bureaucratic oppositions are essentially activities in which people have surmounted the forces operating for stability and have overcome fear, duty to the organization's leadership, habit, propaganda, and/or cooptation. Such data do not provide much information about organizations in which abuse is widespread but overt struggle does not arise.

William James considered habit to be the "flywheel of civilization." Certainly, no habit is so universal as the habit of obedience. Habit, of course, does not explain much, but merely describes the overwhelming tendency of people to act in accordance with the expectations of others and not to violate the social, moral, or legal norms. Disobedience, which is often called deviance by the defenders of authority, is the exception rather than the rule. Obedience to organizations, then, is just an instance of a more general habit which must be broken before opposition to authority can arise. (4) Human habits are learned; they are not, sociobiology notwithstanding, genetically controlled. We are taught obedience from the very first moments of our existence and the lesson is retaught and reinforced by all of the institutions of society. Religious notions of original sin and eternal punishment, political appeals to patriotism and the extraction of oaths, grading systems in education, evaluation procedures in business, and the threat of ostracism are only some of the ways in which obedience is taught.

Now these are the Laws of the Jungle, and many and mighty
are they;

But the head and the hoof of the Law and the haunch and
the hump is - Obey! (5)

Experimental studies by Milgram, although questionable in regard to
validity, provide evidence about how well the law of obedience is learned.
His research indicates that people are so willing to obey authority that they
will inflict pain on others simply because they have been told to do so. (6)
Political philosopher Christian Bay concludes that "most of us have been
trained, as generations of our ancestors have been before us, to obey almost
all laws almost by instinct, and certainly by habit if not by conviction." (7)

The lessons of obedience that are learned in the process of socialization
direct people not to question any authority. The success of the rhetorical
strategy of arguing from authority rather than giving reasons to support
claims and commands indicates the pervasiveness of habits of obedience.
Organizations reap the benefits of the work that other social institutions have
done. The adult associates "ought" with the commands of any authority,
much as Pavlov's dogs associated the bell with food. Unquestioning reverence
for authority figures is learned early in life. Certain authority roles (for
example, the parental) have been crucial to our existence and we have
transferred fear, veneration, and the sense of dependence from them to
authority in general. The vital authorities of our early years, such as parents
and physicians, have had the literal power of life and death over us and it was
in the interest of our peace of mind to regard them as benevolent, to believe
that they had our good at heart. We also tend to generalize these judgments
to all authority figures. The fear of attacking authorities is also based on the
difficulties of withstanding the consequence of the absence of authority:
freedom. When people are not guided by authority they become responsible
for their choices and, as many existentialists have noted, responsibility often
causes anguish.

Habits of obedience may also be related to the establishment of a sense of
loyalty to a formal group. After the manner of Erich Segal's idea of love,
loyalty means "never having to say you're sorry." Slogans such as "my country
right or wrong" and "America - love it or leave it" are examples of attempts
to fabricate loyalty. Advice to employees is redolent with such sentiments:
a newspaper column reads, "Boss Bugs You? Start job-hunting." The
development of a sense of obligation to a hierarchy tends to color one's
evaluation of it. Cognitive dissonance theory predicts that if a person has a
positive attitude toward X (for example, the firm) and X indicates that Y (for
example, a policy) is good, then the person will tend to have a positive
attitude toward Y. Certainly, some people can withstand cognitive
dissonance to a greater degree than others, but the general tendency, at least
among Americans, is towards consistency, particularly when the defining
object is as salient as one's employer. The high saliency of one's job makes it
difficult to stand back and judge it, to achieve role distance, because if the
job is found wanting it would be consistent to judge oneself unfavorably too.
It is not surprising, then, that those who are very subservient to authority also
tend to have a low tolerance for dissonance.

Conformity is closely related to the habit of obedience. When individuals accept the dictates of their circumstances they have no autonomous standard against which those circumstances can be judged. Acquiescence makes criticism impossible and opposition, at least in its initial stages, depends upon criticism. However, once a bureaucratic opposition is underway it may be strengthened by conformity, particularly by the other-directedness described by Riesman et al. in The Lonely Crowd. (8) The "herd mentality" makes stampedes possible so long as there is leadership, which it cannot engender by itself.

La Boétie's second ground for passive obedience is propaganda. He refers to events such as the Roman circuses in which "the ancient dictators so successfully lulled their subjects under the yoke, that the stupefied peoples, fascinated by their pastimes and vain pleasures flashed before their eyes, learned subservience as naively, but not so creditably, as little children learn to read by looking at bright picture books." (9) Contemporary imperial and organizational societies have their functional equivalents of the circuses in televised football, country club golf, lavish expense accounts, and company supplied prostitutes. (10) Propaganda also includes ideological indoctrination. La Boétie writes of the authorities: "They never undertake an unjust policy, even one of some importance, without prefacing it with some pretty speech concerning public welfare and common good." (11) Company newsletters notoriously quote the chairman of the board in this manner, and the training in authority holds, witness the statement of Charles Wilson, a former President of General Motors who became Secretary of Defense, "What's good for General Motors is good for the country." Propaganda also inspires reverence and admiration by the fabrication of mystery. La Boétie noted that "the kings of the Assyrians and even after them those of the Medes showed themselves in public as seldom as possible in order to set up a doubt in the minds of the rabble as to whether they were not in some ways more than man..." (12) The washrooms and dining facilities of bureaucratic organizations, strictly segregated by hierarchical rank, appear to be modern counterparts of social mystery. Behind all such practices lurks the Aesopian assumption that "familiarity breeds contempt." (13) Joined to mystery are hypocritical appeals to democracy or community (pseudo-gemeinschaft). It is difficult to oppose authority figures when there is a widespread feeling that "the boss is such a nice guy it would not be the right thing to hurt him."

The third ground for passive obedience noted by La Boétie is cooptation, in which the hierarchy creates a pyramid of privilege by dispensing material benefits to a small group which develops its own loyal followers by parcelling out a share of its grants, and so on. This strategy, which may be termed "feudalization," generates a hierarchy that mirrors but does not entirely embrace the organization. Feudalization, of course, is in strict violation of the administrative ideal of achievement, and is a last resort because it impinges upon the autonomy of the leadership. It is often difficult to distinguish between reluctance to engage in struggles based on bought loyalty and reluctance based on fear of losing one's position, because where feudalization occurs stable expectations are built up. In organizations, privilege is generally relative to possible privation - the carrot may be more evident, but the stick is more fundamental. The centrality of occupation to self-concept, the general scarcity of employment opportunities, and the negative sanctions that an administration can mete out (for example, geographical transfers, assignments to odious or meaningless tasks, or simply strict enforcement of rules that would make work uncomfortable or intolerable) all make the comparison between opposition to a tyrant and opposition to an organization plausible.

Another more inclusive account of the barriers to opposition is provided by utilitarianism or, as it is called in contemporary social science, exchange theory. (14) In exchange theory what the early modern thinkers called fear and desire is translated into pecuniary terms as cost and benefit. Benefits such as liberty and justice are measured against the costs of opposition, and the decision whether or not to struggle is guided by the cost-benefit ratio (in Homans' terms) or by calculations of net profit or loss. This bourgeois theory (the adjective is used in a descriptive and not in a pejorative sense) is adapted to the culture in which it appears and seems to explain why many people do not oppose organizations in which abuses are widespread. Exchange theory, however, may be more a way in which people justify their opposition or their failure to oppose than a motivator for conduct. In a capitalist society cost-benefit language is publicly acceptable, even when it is difficult or impossible to assign numerical or even ordinal values to the various outcomes.

The costs that enter into the "rational calculus" are varied. In trying to assess the differential success of his recruiting drive, one of the leaders of a bureaucratic opposition in a large law office writes about a secretary: "Even if she felt that the rule was wrong, the fact that she endured it for so long made her want to pass on that rule to others." (15) The cost here was self-esteem; the woman did not want to admit to herself or others that she had suffered for nothing. The leader of the opposition continues: "The two associates who joined our opposition were both unusual in the sense that any hopes for quick partnership opportunities were destroyed." (16) Why did they bear this cost? "They both told me that it wasn't a hard decision. It was a responsible act of freedom." (17) Finally, the eight secretaries who joined did not intend to continue at the firm of more than a few years. "Five were putting their husbands through school, two were working for a down payment on a house and one was working to put herself through college." (18)

The degree of commitment to long-term employment in an organization is important in determining who is most likely to join an opposition, as the example of a bureaucratic opposition in a municipal agency illustrates. All of the members "did not look upon expressing their derogatory view of (the abusive supervisor) as synonymous with cutting their own throats. The mean age for the five was 25 and not one of them had any intention of making a career out of their present employment. ... None would be fazed if after stating their minds, they were asked to permanently leave." (19) The threat of the loss of employment, of course, usually works to dampen opposition. In trying to alter sexually-biased practices in an accounting department, the oppositionists were unable "to recruit the other two females in the office to join forces with us. Their excuse was that with the realities of the recession, we too had better have second thoughts about trying to act like crusaders." (20) An intelligence agency oppositionist analyzed the risks in this manner:

"The fear of such banishment from the warmth and security of 'us' into the coldness and uncertainty of 'them,' the fear of losing the favors of the powers that be, all tend to force 'good' behavior, that is, following the 'company line.' It's that or transfer to a far-away office, a Bureau-type Siberia, or the banishment to the Sheol outside the Bureau." (21)

A potential factor mitigating the cost of opposition for those who fear loss of employment or salary increases is some sort of job security. Thus, one would expect, ceteris paribus, that those with civil service protection, union membership, familial employment, or possession of a scarce and needed skill would be more likely to participate in bureaucratic oppositions. An attempt was made to test this hypothesis by questioning employees of unionized and nonunionized airlines. The results of the research indicated that union membership does not seem to affect participation in a bureaucratic opposition. Furthermore, a majority of respondents felt that union membership would have no influence on such activity. The data, based on responses to questions concerning awareness of abusive policies, suggest that unionized workers tend to assume that it is the union's responsibility, not theirs, to see that things are "done right." (22)

Once a bureaucratic opposition is underway, costs can also be assessed on nonparticipants. An active member of a bureaucratic opposition waged against an airline's new anti-hijacking regulations stated that the seniority and recognized expertise which she and several others possessed influenced those who were unwilling to participate to "go along" if one of the leaders was present: "If anyone disagreed with us, they would not admit it because they felt the group pressure." (23) In this case people participated, were swept into action, because they found it too costly to remain inactive.

Even if each person could affix relative values to the various costs and benefits of opposition, such calculations would be meaningful only for the moment and might be altered drastically with changing circumstances. When a leader of a bureaucratic opposition in a grounds department was asked about how he was able to handle his concern about losing his job if he participated in an effort to change a demeaning policy, he responded: "I was very concerned about keeping my job. I needed it greatly. But I became so enraged at the policy that I simply forgot about my fear." (24) Can his statement be analyzed in exchange theoretical terms to read that the benefit of changing the policy outweighed the cost of possible dismissal? A preferable interpretation is that, for a period of time, he became a non-economic actor, that he acted without calculation.

A modification of the utilitarian exchange theories, which is specifically concerned with whether or not people will participate in political action, appears in Mancur Olsen's The Logic of Collective Action. Olsen argues that rational and self-interested people will not help to achieve common interests except under special conditions, because they will enjoy the benefits whether or not they make sacrifices to bring them about. In order, then, to understand why so many people do participate in collective action it is necessary to assume that human beings are not always instrumentally rational and self-interested, and/or that opposition groups exert various pressures or offer incentives to join them. One may interpret the works of revolutionary theorists such as Mao Tse-Tung and Fidel Castro in a bourgeois fashion, arguing that they offered moral incentives to adjust the balance sheet. Such moral incentives include, as student of rebellions James Downton notes, comradeship, pride, and purpose. (25) In his analysis of various types of groups challenging the polity or the general society, William Gamson comes to a similar conclusion: commitment to a cause allows one to transcend the calculations of cost-benefit analysis. (26)

Narrow-gauge self-interest within the limits defined by a social structure, then, is only one motivation for action. It is "consciousness that does not transcend its rootedness in an economically competitive mode of production." (27) Max Weber was well aware of other varieties of motivated action: "Less 'rational' actions are typed by Weber in terms of the pursuit of 'absolute ends,' as flowing from affectual sentiments, or as 'traditional,' (28) Although Weber tends to associate different types of action with different kinds of collective associations, it is unwarranted to conclude that only one mode of action is present in each type of social structure. Although traditional conduct seems unlikely to motivate oppositions to bureaucratic authority in industrialized societies, action motivated by the pursuit of absolute ends and action impelled by affectual sentiments can and do, together or separately, actuate bureaucratic oppositions.

Attempts to use utilitarian theories to understand why people do not take part in grounded oppositions is further complicated by the complex relations between knowledge and action. The utilitarian theories assume knowledge of abuse and a considered decision about whether to act. However, at least some people are "blind to" or fail to see any abuse, and therefore fail to act. Many theories of falsified or distorted knowledge and conception have tried to account for such blindness. Those concerned with why people do not believe or know what seems to be so obvious to others have coined terms such as happy consciousness, bad faith, false consciousness, repression, mystification, and viciously acquired naivete to describe this phenomenon. Theories of non-knowledge claim that people misinterpret situations either through unconscious distortion or through inattention. Thus, with reference to bureaucratic opposition, one reason why people do not act to correct abuses is that they are unaware of them. While certain structurally grounded abuses may be well hidden in some organizations, the vast majority of abuses are not concealed from employees. Weber indicates that "bureaucratic administration always tends to be an administration of 'secret sessions': insofar as it can, it hides its knowledge and action from criticism." (29) However, Weber is referring to the attempt to keep secrets from the public, not from insiders. The lack of recognition of abuses, then, is most often the result of some process of non-knowledge.

It is not surprising that recognition of organizational abuse is not the same for all of those in similar positions. The psychological and social characteristics of those who say the "emperor has no clothes" are apt to be different than the characteristics of those who are oblivious to the nudity. For example, oppositionists are likely to be recent arrivals to the organization. Young Turks have not been habituated to convention, do not yet have strong loyalties, are potential or actual competitors with older employees, are uncertain about their future, often have standards that they bring with them from another organization, and feel the discomfort of alienation from ongoing informal groups. The experience of the stranger, who is unhindered by the everyday mentality of the natives and "sees" more than they do, is common to new arrivals. Distance from the everyday is also more pronounced in professionals who uphold standards which are explicitly independent of, and often in conflict with, conventional bureaucratic norms. This clash of standards is one of the bases of the tension between administrators and their professional subordinates that has been extensively studied by sociologists. (30) Professionals are expected, in Thoreau's terms, to "march to the beat of a different drummer." For example, social workers who strongly identified with their profession were found to be more likely to deviate from administrative procedures than their less committed colleagues. (31) The "professionalized" social workers justified rule violations in terms of more effective service to their clients. In contrast, welfare workers with weak professional orientation had a greater tendency to follow organization's rules and procedures more strictly.

When people judge that the organization is violating moral and not only bureaucratic standards, they are placed into a condition of role conflict. In such cases the role of employee, which in a bureaucracy prescribes obedience to the commands of superiors, clashes with the more generalized dictates of citizenship, religious faith, or what Weber called ethics of ultimate ends. However, although Weber's idea of ethical autonomy makes role conflict intelligible, his own discussion avoids the issue by resolving it in favor of obedience to hierarchical command:

An official who, according to his own view, receives an order that is wrong can - and should - raise protests. However, if the superordinated office persists in its instructions, then it is not only his duty but his Honor to carry them out in such a manner as if they were in agreement with his own convictions, and thereby show that his sense of duty to office outweighs his own willfulness. (32)

For Weber, the politician is of a different species or spirit than the bureaucrat. He writes:

... it is immensely moving when a mature man - no matter whether young or old in years - is aware of a responsibility for the consequences of his conduct and really feels such responsibility with heart and soul. He then acts by following an ethic of responsibility and somewhere he reaches the point where he says: 'Here I stand; I can do no other.' (33)

One way of resolving role conflicts is to compartmentalize one's roles. "In modern societies, marked by a high degree of space and time specialization and separation of human activities, it is possible for someone to be one person at certain places and times and another person at other places and times." (34) By employing this schizoid tactic one fails to see the immoral actions for what they are (moral standards are reserved for roles which are not enacted in the bureaucracy). In his advice to clinical psychologists, Ernest Keen acknowledges the phenomenon of compartmentalization. He warns

To become aware of his own experience of self-as-subject may enlighten latent values. This may put him into agonizing conflict between his personal values and his bureaucratic values, and the therapist must be willing to accept responsibility for his role in bringing that conflict to a head. (35)

Even in cases in which abuses are recognized, there are barriers to participation in bureaucratic oppositions that do not reflect the operation of the "rational calculus." For example, Western sex-role norms inhibit opposition by divorcing means from motive. Men are expected to be active and aggressive, but they are also supposed to be "toughminded," to be insensitive to personal feelings and morality, and to direct their attention to the "bottom line." Women, in contrast, are supposed to be "tenderminded" (attentive to feeling and morality), but they are also expected to be passive and quiescent. Thus, the male role permits the means to opposition but not the motive, and the female role permits the motive but not the means. Particular individuals, of course, do not always act consistently with either their own normative standards or social role expectations.

Aside from the barriers to opposition imposed by deep-rooted roles is an often unreasoned cynicism with regard to the importance and probable success of one's efforts, and a resulting ignorance of the appropriate means of making changes. In a study of American soldiers done during World War II about one-half of the sample questioned indicated that during their career in the army they had felt the desire to bring a complaint to the attention of the authorities. Four-fifths of these people failed to bring any complaints and cited as reasons for their decisions:
1. difficulty in gaining access to the Inspector General (the officer who performed the role of trouble-shooter);
2. the judgment that it was futile even to try to do anything;
3. fear of reprisals. (36)
Whether or not cynicism is justified depends upon the circumstances of the particular case, but that it engenders ignorance of the effective means of opposition is unquestionable. (37) When courses of action are not institutionalized and when examples of them are not well known, they will not, ceteris paribus, be frequently pursued. In representative democracies the party system provides a form of institutionalized opposition, while revolutionary strategists have many blueprints and historical examples. Oppositional action within organizations has neither ongoing institutions to express it nor a historical tradition to support it - there is not even a term in the language for such action.

Bureaucratic opposition, of course, is not the only way in which a person can respond to disagreement with organizational policies or practices. Disagreement with organizational authority creates conflict and conflict can be resolved in many ways. Kurt Singer, in a decades-old article, made a persuasive case that there are four basic solutions to conflict based on the two dimensions of cognition and volition. (38) The first or cognitive dimension poses the alternatives of acknowledgment or repudiation of the conflict. The second or volitional dimension poses the alternatives of active or passive response to the cognition. Repudiation of conflict coupled with passivity means isolation from the field of activity. In an organization such isolation would involve either psychological withdrawal from one's job (lowering its saliency in one's life) or actually quitting. Passive acknowledgment of conflict means admitting defeat before any struggle is initiated, renouncing one's objectives: it is following the advice of "suffer and be still." This resolution is widespread and may account for high rates of absenteeism, lackadaisical work habits, and feelings of alienation and hostility. Such symptoms, including expressive acts of sabotage, are the result of partial resignation, the incomplete resolution of the conflict situation. A secretary writes, "And everywhere we rebelled in a thousand small ways - taking extra time in the ladies' room, misfiling important letters, 'forgetting' to correct typos." (39)

Repudiation of conflict coupled with an activist disposition leads to behavior that attempts to modify the conflict situation, to integrate in some way the opposing positions: it is the strategy of compromise that draws so much praise from mainstream administrative theorists, though its particular expressions may be mildly subversive. There are several ways in which employees may attempt to compromise a conflict situation. If a policy or superior prescribes violations of bureaucratic or moral norms the employee may obey sporadically, agreeing to the order but doing the "right" thing when the boss is not looking. A similar strategy is for the employee to try to compensate for the undesirable consequences in some way. For example, a secretary whose boss ordered her to give him monies from petty cash to use for his personal expenses replaced the funds from her own salary. Similarly, when a welfare department's policy changed and no longer allowed certain expenditures for home furnishings, a case worker would write up a report in which monies that were actually to be spent for furnishings would be charged to some allowable category. Another variant of compromise is the effort of a subordinate to "patch things up" with a client who has been abused by a superior. Bordering on more acute acknowledgment of conflict are forms of unproclaimed resistance. For example, when there is a directive to crack down on time spent for lunch, workers may begin to take only an hour instead of their usual hour and fifteen minutes for the official 45 minute break. On the whole, the development of informal rules arises from the compromise tactic of conflict resolution. (40) Many rulings, of course, cannot be compromised and the efforts of employees towards compromise are frequently feeble attempts to assuage guilt.

The last resolution of conflict, in which incompatibility is actively acknowledged, is termed by Singer "resolute contention": When a person "does not want the clash of antagonistic forces to be eschewed, attenuated or denied, he takes his stand and decides to fight the conflict out...." (41) It is within this category of resolute contention that bureaucratic oppositions fall. They require both full recognition of incompatible rules and a decision to fight to establish the situation that "should" obtain.

Individuals do not randomly select one of Singer's four conflict resolution strategies. The choice among the alternatives is influenced by a number of factors, some of which are personality, the actions taken by others, and prior experience with and expectations of the organization's probable responses. Political scientists have been concerned with determining how those who participate in political activities differ from those who do not enter the fray. They distinguish among levels of participation (whether or not the person performs a leadership role) and among types of groups (traditional, democratic, or extremist). Lester Milbrath, for example, studied research on behavior directed towards affecting the "decisional outcomes of government." He concluded that those enacting such behavior tend to have above average education and socioeconomic position, a sense of political efficacy, a sense of political duty, self-confidence, and above average knowledge and sophistication. In addition, participants are more likely to be male, sociable and outgoing, and not cynical. (42)

The extent to which participation in the political system is similar to involvement in a bureaucratic opposition is difficult to assess. Impressionistic conclusions based on the case data collected for this study indicate that those who are most active in bureaucratic opposition groups have characteristics similar to Milbrath's intensive participants. In addition, bureaucratic oppositionists tend to be concerned with the ethical dimensions of existence. The sociological and political science literature on "extremist" group members does not seem to be applicable to bureaucratic oppositions.

The preceding discussion has been concerned with the conditions inhibiting opposition as they are expressed in the individual. There are also strictly social conditions that block opposition which are, perhaps, reflective of individual motives when they are woven into group traditions. Within organizations, informal groups and their orientation to the formal authority structure are factors with considerable influence on the probability of struggle. In general, informal work groups are functionally adapted to the organization and provide their members with ways of coping within the boundaries of the administrative order. They are usually conservative forces because they make the workplace more personal and less distant, anonymous, and threatening. Their ideologies preach "live and let live," and although they may disparage the organization and its leaders they offer no proposals for change. There are, however, "deviant" informal groups which are positive conditions for opposition. In such groups there is a tradition or a culture of active opposition to authority. When this rate type of informal group exists it may have developed from past experiences with bureaucratic oppositions in which the possibilities for success were demonstrated. Despite the possibility of oppositional traditions, however, the vast majority of informal work groups negatively affect the potential for opposition. Their collective attitude is one of indifference or open hostility to any change. It is only when the policy which may provide the ground for an opposition is newly instituted, and particularly when it disrupts the informal group's adaptation to the organization, that such a group is likely to become oppositional. An example of a disruptive policy is a no-talking rule which interferes with the group's sociability function.

The structure of informal groups and their traditions are important because bureaucratic oppositions are best pursued when several employees participate. There have, of course, been both successful and unsuccessful one-person oppositions and they will be discussed in some detail in the following chapter. However, it is easier for an oppositionist not to go it alone for both tactical and emotional reasons. More participants generally means more resources such as ideas, knowledge, and contacts within and outside the hierarchy. For example, an opposition group of nurses felt strengthened by the presence of a nurse who was romantically linked with a medical staff member, even though he was already married. (43) Also, because the administrative myth claims that all policy is rational, any opposition is almost automatically suspected of irrationality. Lone oppositionists are often tagged as "mental cases," deviants, or troublemakers, and are not taken seriously. It is more difficult to make charges of mental imbalance when two or more people publicly acknowledge the same abuse. Generally, bureaucratic oppositions that are one-man shows are so only because no allies could be found. There is almost always a search for allies, if only to fortify the resolve and corroborate the judgment of the lone oppositionist. Also, the search for allies may be motivated by a desire to avoid pariah status.

Large-scale social opposition groups, termed "challenge groups" by Gamson, tend to be increasingly effective with greater membership. Such is not the case for bureaucratic oppositions which, except in special cases of oppositions to unions or other formally democratic structures, seem to depend upon face-to-face interaction. Where representative institutions exist attempts can be made to organize electoral support, but where they do not exist there is usually a necessity for tight solidarity. Between 12 and 15 members seems to be an upper limit for oppositions, and many of the groups contain only four or five people. Of course, the pool from which opposition group members can be drawn also affects the size of the group, as does the level of authority against which the opposition is raised.

The development and maintenance of the opposition group, and not only its actual strategies, require great effort. Since groups do not form abruptly and spontaneously like mushrooms after a rain, it is necessary to mobilize and unite those who may be willing to act. Mobilization depends upon the existence of quasi-groups which may be transformed into self-conscious collectivities. The process of transformation has been described by Morris Ginsberg who stated that a quasi-group is a collectivity which has "no recognizable structure, but whose members have certain interests or modes of behavior in common which may at any time lead them to form themselves into definite groups." (44) There are many quasi-groups in organizations, some of which crosscut one another. The most obvious are formed by people who are in the same organizational position, such as dock loaders, nurses, social workers, accounting clerks, or, more generally, the subordinates of a certain official. Crosscutting groups may be based on ethnicity, sex, age, religion, or political affiliation (more generally, upon any nonoccupational interest), and whether or not they are activated depends a great deal on external social circumstances.

In addition to quasi-groups and, probably more important, are the informal work groups discussed above. Despite their generally conservative function within organizations, it is possible for informal groups sometimes to be transformed into oppositions, which is probably why they have both fascinated and scared apologists for the administrative ideal since the Depression. (45) The leader of the dock worker's opposition described earlier analyzed the development of his opposition group from an informal work group: "The workers in our area had gotten to be a close-knit group, because of all the talking and joking we had done. It's possible that is why talking and joking aren't allowed." (46)

The recruitment into bureaucratic oppositions is usually gradual because it involves risks and the testing of loyalties on all sides. Likely prospects for participation are those who indulge in the griping and black humor that is the first response to abuse. Although such activities are useful for spreading discontent and for delegitimating authorities, they do not themselves constitute opposition. Depending upon the circumstances, group formation may result from the exasperation with a long train of abuses or may be directly related to a single precipitating event. Different members of the group may have based their decision to struggle on different grounds (in response to different abuses). Initiation into the group is informal. "Hey, you know, we ought to do something about that" is often sufficient inducement to participate for those who are already motivated. Formal groups have initiation procedures which tend to be elaborate and replete with ritual, and which function to inform everyone that the recruit is unmistakably a member. For example, military induction ceremonies are blatant and include shaving the heads of recruits, tagging them with metal identification plates, and outfitting them distinctively, all of which is reminiscent of cattle branding. Initiations into fraternal and religious groups also are filled with instances of ceremonial investment. Such practices function to reinforce the newcomer's commitment to the group and to make resignation difficult.

Informal groups, which generally lack initiation ceremonies, are continually threatened by casual participation and "dropping out" by members. There is no need for members to explain publicly why they have not participated fully, they have no gifts to return, and there are no legal proceedings for detachment. To bolster solidarity, noninstitutionalized pressures must be mobilized. For example, frequent face-to-face interaction among members, especially when it includes conversation about the organization's abuses, serves to maintain and enhance commitment. When others within the organization are aware of the group's existence the solidarity of its members is often enhanced and is sometimes intensified when members are stigmatized and ostracized by nonmembers. (47) In reciprocal fashion, those who are potential converts to the group but who have refused to join are usually viewed negatively by the group's members. At times the hostility of the group against outsiders becomes more important to it than the original goal of change. And when the opposition is terminated, whether or not it has been successful, these hostilities tend to endure.

Commitment to the group need not be based only on affirmation of its goal, but may also be based on personal loyalties. Personal loyalty is a general characteristic of primary groups, which are characterized by gemeinschaft (relations are personal and diffuse rather than specific to a certain role). Where oppositions are based on gesellschaft (self-interested exchange), there is often some unwritten bargain in which individual members receive something of value as an inducement to maintain their participation. Such rewards vary from the opportunity to exert power to "getting a piece of the action" (for example, being next in line for promotion to the position whose current incumbent is under attack by the oppositionists). When people become disenchanted with the issue that engendered opposition, despairing of victory or simply becoming annoyed with all the time oppositional activity takes away from other pursuits, their active commitment is supported by solidarity. In their analysis of the German Army's performance during World War II, Shils and Janowitz claimed that the higher echelons miscalculated the source of the soldier's commitment to keep fighting under adverse conditions. It was assumed by the military command that patriotism and a faith in the nobility of Hitler's mission was sufficient to sustain commitment. Shils and Janowitz indicate that, on the contrary, loyalty was accorded mainly to the soldier's small unit, to the individuals who comprised this primary group. (48)

The formation of groups that do not have high status in their social environment, to which people find it risky to belong and which do not have legitimacy, is hindered by the difficulties in developing trust among potential members. Group formation is made even more difficult by the atmosphere of competition engendered by organizations, in which people vie with one another for advancement and privileges. Competitive relations and the alienation that accompanies them create undercurrents of mistrust and suspicion which are difficult to overcome. A leader of a secretarial opposition comments, "This hatred of other women, which was really self-hatred, made it easy for the Editor-in-Chief to divide and conquer." (49)

When people may face being fired or fired upon if their active opposition is publicly known, developing trust poses problems as acute as reaching the decision to fight to make changes in the organization. Once there is trust, however, high risk serves to foster commitment because each one feels an obligation not to let the others down. The positive relation between risk and commitment, noted by Downton in his study of rebel groups, (50) may also be explained by cognitive dissonance theory as a result of our tendency to feel positive effect for that which we must suffer to achieve. (51) In part, this explanation covers the patriotism of war veterans, the loyalty of hazed fraternity brothers, and the love of a mother for her infant. Many bureaucratic oppositions, however, are not very risky. Pledges of "united we stand, divided we fall" and frank admissions of the risks involved in struggle are often sufficient to create a trust which extends as far as the organizational roles, but which does not involve the whole person. Once such trust is established among members of an opposition group there is rarely any further mention of the risks.

Even where trust has been created there is still a problem of maintaining commitment. Gamson indicates that

> bureaucratic organization helps a group with the problem of pattern maintenance. By creating a structure of the roles with defined expectations in the place of diffuse commitments, a challenging group can better assure that certain necessary tasks will be routinely performed. (52)

Bureaucratic opposition groups, however, rarely become formal organizations themselves because they are usually small, face-to-face groups whose members believe (not always correctly) that their struggle will last for only a short time. Sometimes the informality of oppositions promotes their success, because the administrative authorities often prefer a well-organized adversary to loose congeries of disgruntled individuals. Organized oppositions, as Simmel recognized, are more predictable, can be more easily coopted, and can more readily arrange compromises than informal groups:

> ... against a diffuse multitude of enemies, one gains more often particular victories, but has great difficulty in achieving decisive actions which definitely fix the mutual relationship of the forces. (53)

Basic to the organization of a group is its degree of centralization and the nature of its leadership. Most ongoing groups have specific procedures for selecting leaders. For example, elections are used in democracies, accession in monarchies, and preemption in revolutionary governments. Small groups that are formed independently of the directives of authorities often use the method of assumption in which the one assumed by all to be the best qualified becomes the leader. To the extent to which bureaucratic opposition groups are centralized and can be said to have leaders, assumption is the dominant method of leadership selection. However, the infrequency of oppositional activity makes it difficult to judge leadership ability. Unlike the hunting groups of the Bushmen, in which the most skilled hunter is the leader who deploys men to different areas and tasks, bureaucratic opposition groups cannot base selection of a leader on instrumentally rational criteria. Perhaps this is one reason why bureaucratic oppositions often have no clearly defined administration and why those that do have leaders have no formal procedures for acknowledging them. Generalizing from the data, leaders of opposition groups have two basic characteristics: they are highly articulate and they are the most strongly or among the most strongly motivated to achieve the group's goal. Taking liberties with Weber's categories, the authority of these leaders is based on charisma. Their personal influence alone determines the extent to which they will be heeded. They have no reservoir of force with which to compel obedience. Like all unofficial leaders they must consult far more than command. Leaders of bureaucratic oppositions serve as advisers, coordinators, and planners, provided that others are willing to listen to them. Such noncoercive administration is frequent among small groups and even characterizes whole communities such as the Northern Algonquians, the Kalahari Bushmen, and some Eskimo. These communities are characterized by primary interaction, low population density, and relatively simple social organization.

Leaderless bureaucratic opposition groups differ very little from those with leaders. In the former, advice is more readily given by and taken from those who have special-area competence, and, thus, most of the members of the group are at some time in positions of leadership. (54) Lack of centralization is not only due to the small size and expected brief duration of the opposition, but to the relative status of and risks taken by the members. Most often all the members of the opposition group are at the same level of the organizational hierarchy and, therefore, confront similar risks. When subordinates and their immediate superiors unite, the latter usually become the leaders. For example, in academic bureaucratic oppositions those who have tenure tend to take the lead and to expose themselves to the authorities of the university more than do the untenured faculty who face the risk that their contracts will not be renewed.

When bureaucratic oppositions are expected to last for an extended period of time (more than a few weeks) and/or when large numbers of people are involved in them, organizational complexity develops. Specific roles are created and filled, including leadership positions. Examples of highly complex opposition groups are found most frequently in labor unions. Not only are unions legally required to have a democratic form, but they were initiated as a kind of bureaucratic opposition and maintain a mythology of struggle and organization. Also, oppositions against union authority often require the coordination of large numbers of people. The wildcat strikes by mine workers in Appalachia, which lasted for several months during the summer of 1977 and which were directed primarily against the United Mine Workers, exemplify a highly complex opposition group in action. The fact that workers were scattered among numerous sites throughout the regional required centralized planning and coordination. The event that precipitated the opposition was a change in medical benefits, which had been free in the past but which were then put on a fee basis. Comments made by the miners, however, indicated that the precipitant was only the straw that broke the camel's back: the oppositionists accused the union of being generally indifferent to the needs of the workers. The wildcat strike included about one-half of the UMW's 175,000 working members and it appeared that the organization of the opposition was based in some of the UMW district offices. (55) The most militant district, #17 in Charleston, West Virginia, was treated by the UMW hierarchy as a kind of "bargaining agent" for all of the strikers, although it had not been authorized to speak for the other districts. Oppositions against unions, such as this wildcat strike, are on the borderline between bureaucratic oppositions and traditional political processes because they may involve actions against a federated body by some of its legally constituted parts.

Another complex bureaucratic opposition group is the Professional Drivers' Council (PROD, Inc.) which has been in conflict with its union, the International Brotherhood of Teamsters, since 1971. Membership figures vary, but in 1977 PROD claimed 10,000 members, of whom 4,000 had paid the $20 yearly dues. PROD has charged that the top officials of the Teamsters have been financially irresponsible, have failed to push for legislation and contract agreements which would reduce safety hazards, and have made a mockery of union democracy. Unlike the UMW wildcatters, whose opposition arose within the union's formal structure, PROD was inspired by Ralph Nader's public interest group, from which it became independent after a year of tutelage. The diversity and complexity of PROD's activities preclude a simple structure for the group. It has won court cases which the Teamsters' grievance committees had refused to fight and it has lobbied the Departments of Transportation, Justice, and Labor, and the Internal Revenue Service. PROD also publishes books and a "hard-hitting" bi-monthly newspaper which recounts the actions of its members and Teamster retaliations. (56) Finally, the organization has been a literal prod, holding meetings throughout the United States in which teamsters are informed about how to clean up their local unions.

Despite the publicity that they get, large and complex bureaucratic opposition groups are anomalies. Most oppositions are small, leaderless, face-to-face groups in which any specialized activity is done on an ad hoc basis and is generally volunteered. The strict discipline of a revolutionary party is only needed in those few instances in which there are risks of violence. Such extreme risks seem to be restricted to bureaucracies that have the means to use violence, such as the police and, for different reasons relating to their bloody origins, some unions. In many oppositions internal conflicts arise from personality clashes and differences of opinion about tactics. Such conflicts may actually benefit the opposition as different people test out their own lines of offense. The benefits of a multiplicity of tactics in bureaucratic oppositions contrast sharply with the need for discipline in societal challenge groups. (57) However, even large-scale social movements may benefit from a diversity in the challenge groups that compose them. For example, the black movement seems to have benefited from the blend of violent tactics and threats (Student Nonviolent Coordinating Committee and the Black Panthers), legal action (National Association for the Advancement of Colored People, NAACP), and moral persuasion and example (Martin Luther King, Jr. and the Southern Christian Leadership Conference).

The formation and coordination of individuals into opposition groups are the result of the interplay between the ever-present grounds for struggle and the organizational conditions which inhibit dissent. That the countervailing conditions against conflict can be overcome is evidenced by the appearance of oppositions, but that these conditions pose difficult obstacles is shown by the usually transient duration, localized scope, face-to-face nature, and lack of division of labor of opposition groups. At times, of course, group formation does not occur and an individual decides to go it alone. Energies spent in mobilizing an opposition group to attempt to change policies or rule-violating personnel only form the prelude to bureaucratic opposition itself. The actual struggle must proceed according to a strategy or course of action through which the oppositionists attempt to achieve their goal of instituting desired changes. Such strategies and the tactics derived from them form the subject matter of the following section.

CHAPTER 3: NOTES

(1) Thomas Hobbes, Leviathan, New York: E.P. Dutton, 1950.

(2) Talcott Parsons, The Structure of Social Action, Glencoe: Free Press, 1949, p. 93.

(3) Étienne de La Boétie, The Politics of Obedience: The Discourse of Voluntary Servitude, New York: Free Life Editions, 1975, p. 60. Parsons would not disagree; he claims that naked power is a most costly means for securing order, and favors the less physical means of shared norms.

(4) However, one recognizes that many abuses themselves are acts of disobedience on the part of superiors.

(5) Rudyard Kipling, refrain from "The Law of the Jungle."

(6) Stanley Milgram, Obedience to Authority: An Experimental View, New York: Harper and Row, 1974; for a critique of this work, see for example, Martin Wenglinsky, "Review of Milgram: Obedience to Authority," Contemporary Sociology: A Journal of Reviews 4 (November, 1975), 613-17.

(7) Christian Bay, "Civil Disobedience: Prerequisite for Democracy in Mass Society," pp. 222-242 in Donald W. Hanson and Robert Booth Fowler (eds.), Obligation and Dissent: An Introduction to Politics, Boston: Little, Brown and Co., p. 224.

(8) David Riesman, et al., The Lonely Crowd: A Study of the Changing American Character, Garden City: Doubleday, 1950.

(9) La Boétie, op. cit., p. 70.

(10) For example, legal testimony revealed that "Bell employees were used as procurers to secure women for high officials in American Telephone and Telegraph Co.," and these services were eventually paid for by telephone customers. ("Bell Testimony tells Procurer Role," Chicago Sun-Times (August 16, 1977), 18)

(11) La Boétie, op. cit., p. 71.

(12) Ibid., p. 72.

(13) Aesop, "The Fox and the Lion."

(14) See, for example, the work of Peter Blau (Exchange and Power in Social Life, New York: John Wiley, 1964) and George Homans (Social Behavior, New York: Harcourt, Brace and World, 1961).

(15) Student paper D.J.M, 1976, p. 13.

(16) Ibid.

(17) Ibid.

(18) Ibid.

(19) Student paper M.H., 1976, p. 10.

(20) Student paper F.J., 1976, pp. 2-3.

(21) Student paper K.K., 1977, p. 14.

(22) Edie Zukauskas, "Research Methods Paper," 1977.

(23) Student paper, E.K., 1976

(24) Interview L.P., 1977.

(25) James V. Downton Jr., Rebel Leadership: Commitment and Charisma in the Revolutionary Process, New York: Free Press, 1973, p. 62.

(26) William A. Gamson, The Strategy of Social Protest, Homewood, Illinois: Dorsey Press, 1974, p. 111.

(27) Lewis A. Coser, Continuities in the Study of Social Conflict, New York: Free Press, 1967, p. 145.

(28) Max Weber, "The Social Psychology of the World Religions," pp. 267-301 in From Max Weber: Essays in Sociology, H.H. Gerth and C. Wright Mills (eds.), New York: Oxford University Press, 1946, pp. 295 ff.

(29) Max Weber, "Bureaucracy," pp. 196-244 in Gerth and Mills, op. cit., p. 233.

(30) The following works discuss the tension of professionals in bureaucracies: George A. Miller, "Professionals in Bureaucracy: Alienation Among Industrial Scientists and Engineers," American Sociological Review 32 (October 1967), 755-68; Barney Glaser, "The Local-Cosmopolitan Scientist," American Journal of Sociology 69 (November 1963), 246-60; Proshanta K. Nandi, "Career and Life Organization of Professionals: A Study of Contrasts Between College and University Professors," (Ph.D. dissertation, University of Minnesota, 1968).

(31) Peter M. Blau and W. Richard Scott, Formal Organizations: A Comparative Approach, San Francisco: Chandler, 1962.

(32) Max Weber, "Parlament und Regierung im Neugeordneten Deutchland," quoted in Ralph P. Hummel, The Bureaucratic Experience, New York: St. Martin's Press, 1977, pp. 95-96.

(33) Weber, Max, "Politics as a Vocation," p. 127 in Gerth and Mills (eds.), op. cit.

(34) Deena Weinstein and Michael A. Weinstein, Roles of Man: An Introduction to the Social Sciences, Hinsdale, Illinois: Dryden Press, 1972, p. 178. See pages 169-186 in this book for a discussion of compartmentalization and other techniques of dealing with such role conflicts.

(35) Ernest Keen, Three Faces of Being: Toward an Existentialist Clinical Psychology, New York: Appleton-Century-Crofts, 1970, pp. 331-32.

(36) Samuel A. Stouffer et al., The American Soldier Volume I: Adjustment During Army Life, Princeton: Princeton University Press, 1949, pp. 99-100.

(37) The more bureaucratic oppositions are reported in the media, the more likely that people will be acquainted with various strategies to adapt to their particular situation.

(38) Kurt Singer, "The Resolution of Conflict," Social Research 16, #2 (June 1949), 230-45.

(39) Judith Ann, "The Secretarial Proletariat," pp. 86-100 in Robin Morgan (ed.), Sisterhood is Powerful: An Anthology of Writings from the Women's Movement, New York: Random House, 1970, p. 100.

(40) Primary work groups, not only individuals, create informal rules as a compromise tactic to resolve conflict. For an analysis of this response with regard to inefficient policies see Donald Roy, "Efficiency and 'The Fix': Informal Intergroup Relations in a Piecework Machine Shop," American Journal of Sociology 60 (1955), 225-266.

(41) Singer, op. cit., p. 239.

(42) Lester Milbrath, Political Participation: How and Why do People Get Involved in Politics?, Chicago: Rand McNally, 1965, pp. 48-89.

(43) Student paper D.B., 1977, p. 4.

(44) Morris Ginsberg, Sociology, London: Oxford University Press, 1953, p. 40.

(45) For the early work on informal work groups see, for example, F.J. Roethlisberger and William J. Dickson, Management and the Worker, Cambridge: Harvard University Press, 1939.

(46) Student paper S.A., 1976, p. 10.

(47) This process is seen too in political rebellion groups; see Downton, op. cit., p. 70.

(48) Edward A. Shils and Morris Janowitz, "Cohesion and Disintegration in the Wehrmacht in World War II," Public Opinion Quarterly 12 (Summer 1948): 280-315.

(49) Judith Ann, "The Secretarial Proletariat," op. cit., p. 95.

(50) Downton, op. cit.

(51) Research on experimentally created small groups to test this thesis indicates confidence in it. See for example, Elliott Aronson and Judson Mills, "The Effect of Severity of Initiation on Liking for a Group," Journal of Abnormal and Social Psychology 59 (1959), 117-181.

(52) Gamson, op. cit., p. 91.

(53) Peter A. Lawrence, Georg Simmel: Sociologist and European, New York: Harper and Row, 1976, p. 147.

(54) This type of group has been well studied. For a description of some of the results see W.J.H. Sprott, Human Groups, Baltimore: Penguin Books, 1958, especially pp. 153-54.

(55) Helen Dewar, "Temporary Halt in Wildcat Strike Ordered by UMW," Washington Post (August 23, 1977), 1,4.

(56) James Strong, "Teamster 'Ripoff' Charged: Dissidents Assail 'Sky High' Salaries Paid Union Officials," Chicago Tribune (May 28, 1976), 1, 19; and William Ringle, "Teamsters Find Rebels Growing," Lafayette Journal and Courier (July 31, 1977), D-7.

(57) Gamson, op. cit., p. 93.

4 Strategies and Tactics

> Every public action which is not customary, either is wrong or,
> if it is right, is a dangerous precedent. It follows that nothing
> should ever be done for the first time.
> - F.M. Cornford, Microcosmo-
> graphia Academica, vii

Bureaucratic opposition is a political phenomenon that appears in an administrative entity, which is defined so as to exclude politics. According to the myth of administration, each employee has a prescribed role, the performance of which is instrumental to the achievement of the organization's purposes. Under ideal circumstances there is no conflict between the performance of a role and the efficient achievement of official organizational goals. Each employee is assumed to be competent, motivated to perform the prescribed function, and able to contribute to the overall purpose. When any of these assumptions are not met, and they are never met completely, there is a possibility for opposition to business as usual. As Locke pointed out in the Second Treatise, there are always abundant excuses for revolt in any political situation, there are always grounds for opposition. The ideal organization is no less a utopia than the ideal state.

As noted previously, bureaucracies resemble authoritarian states because they do not provide for legitimate and institutionalized opposition. Opposition parties and interest groups in democracies need not legitimate themselves because they are acknowledged to be integral components of the ongoing system. Bureaucratic oppositions are, by definition, outside of and subversive to the system in which they appear and must legitimate themselves. The grounding of oppositions, described in the second chapter, can be conceived of as a process of seeking for justification under conditions in which, according to official definition, justification is ruled out. The task of bureaucratic opposition is to create itself as a legitimate phenomenon.

The grounds for bureaucratic opposition are sought in deviations from or infractions of the norms of the organization itself or the norms of the wider society. Although the members of an opposition may have multiple and even conflicting motives for their participation, they must usually espouse the cause of making the organization live up to its own standards or the standards of the wider social environment. Only if an opposition is carried out secretly can its members avoid the problem of justifying their dissent. However, the grounding of an opposition merely gives it an ideology; it does not make a place for it within the system and certainly does not insure its success. As noted in the third chapter, oppositionists must make a self-conscious commitment to challenge business as usual. They must organize, or at least take individual risks. Bureaucracies are, in one respect, hierarchies of authority. Opposition within them is a threat to the exercise of authority and will nearly always be perceived by officials as a signal that control is giving way to chaos. As in all authoritarian situations, the first concern of officials is that obedience be maintained. In general, oppositionists must walk softly and carry as big a stick as possible. Yet just because their activity is not legitimate they cannot lower their voices, and just because they lack authority they have little clout. Bureaucratic oppositions, then, will predictably meet the resistance of the official hierarchy. Higher officials, who become or are made aware of dissent, will be concerned not merely with the validity of the grounds, but with the maintenance of obedience, submission, and the semblance of order. The oppositionists, however, are often unaware of or, to use Royce's expression, "viciously naive" about the resistance they will meet and the reprisals that they may suffer. Often they believe that the "facts" will speak for themselves, that if only the officials are made cognizant of abuses the abuses will be corrected. Without such innocence or naivete there would be fewer oppositions undertaken. Often the belief that the "facts speak for themselves" is the vital lie that fuels opposition, at least in its initial stages. The oppositionists not only use the norms of the organization or the society to justify their case, but they often believe that the higher administrators are committed to these norms, even to the exclusion of maintaining the appearance of control and wisdom. Such belief is almost never warranted. As Serpico found, the authorities themselves may be corrupt. However, even if they are generally honest, they will feel threatened by breaches in the chain of command. The initial innocence of many oppositionists is, of course, instrumental to their taking action. They are concerned with rectifying a perceived abuse, so concerned that they put on blinders and fail to take the role of the authorities. It is frequently their innocence or naivete that allows them to overcome bureaucratic inertia and to transcend the paradox of their powerlessness. Although they are engaged in a political activity, a combat, they often do not interpret the organization as a political system, and thus are as much as or more victims of the administrative myth than their superiors.

Just because oppositions are not legitimate phenomena within bureaucracies they are relatively unstructured activities. There is no culturally-prescribed role for the oppositionist, no ready-made routine for successful dissent. Highly organized social acts, such as those undertaken by bureaucracies, may be described as linear, sequential, and ordered because they are patterned by a preordained plan. Of course, bureaucracies are not as orderly as their handbooks have it, or else, for one thing, oppositions would not occur. However, business as usual in a bureaucracy often approximates the official plan. The Platonic illusion that form structures content cannot be maintained in any sense for bureaucratic oppositions. Their grounds are not given to them by a charter, but must be sought and created, often in the very process of conflict. Even when the grounds are clear, the oppositionists must devise ways of effecting their goals, must innovate strategies.

The use of the term "strategy" implies a situation of combat. The word is derived from the Greek and originally meant the "art of the general." Its use in the present discussion implies a judgment that the nature of political activity is combative. In the Western tradition, the idea that politics is essentially conflict is paralleled by the idea that it is or should be a rational discussion aimed at determining the common good. The political scientist Maurice Duverger writes:

> Ever since men have been reflecting on politics they have oscillated between two dramatically opposed interpretations. According to one, politics is conflict, a struggle in which power allows those who possess it to ensure their hold on society and to profit by it. According to the other view, politics is an effort to bring about the rule of order and justice in which power guarantees the general interest and the common good against the pressures of private interests. (1)

The two definitions of politics tend to become confused with one another in bureaucratic oppositions. The oppositionists often believe initially that they can effect the changes that they seek merely by appealing rationally to a supposed normative consensus. In later stages, if such stages occur, they frequently shift to the view that politics is a power struggle or at least to the idea that power is a key factor in winning the debate over just what constitutes the common good. In the present discussion, the use of the term strategy is meant to stress the judgment that even when the oppositionists do not believe that they are engaged in combat, the element of conflict, of the military campaign and the adversary relation, is always present. The mere act of "speaking the truth to power" is a combative act because the official who receives the message and is responsible for the organization's proper function is implicitly being accused of dereliction of duty. He or she should have spotted the incompetent or unjust employee, or should not have tolerated the ineffective or immoral policy. Oppositionists, of course, are often unaware that they are mounting such an attack, so involved are they with their cause.

The idea that politics is a rational discussion about the public good implies that the participants in the discussion are equals whose arguments are judged by their intrinsic merits. In the words of Jurgen Habermas, rational politics implies an "ideal speech situation," in which each member is concerned to determine truth and goodness, not to maintain a chain of command or to gain power and privilege. The Machiavellian definition of politics as the act of gaining and maintaining power is more appropriate to the study of bureaucratic opposition than the Platonic idea of rational discourse because the oppositionists are not equal participants in the political process and they confront authorities who are concerned primarily with maintaining order. There is no judgment made in the present discussion about what politics should be, but only about what politics in bureaucracies have been.

The dynamics of a bureaucratic opposition can, in its most general form, be viewed as developing goals, designing strategies for implementing the goals, and enacting strategically appropriate tactical maneuvers. "One can say that tactics is fighting and strategy is planning where and how to fight, with the 'how' construed so as to exclude the details." (2) The goals of a bureaucratic opposition are related to the grounds of the opposition but are not always determined by them. At one extreme the actual goal of an opposition may be the perpetuation of an illegal activity, such as pilferage, while the public ground is the supposed incompetence of a supervisor. At the other extreme the actual goal may follow directly from the ground, as when the oppositionists attempt to remove a rule that causes inefficient or ineffective functioning. Most oppositions fall between the two extremes. First, the members of the opposition may have widely different goals, some of which follow from ungrounded motives and others of which are based on commitment to the public grounds. Second, there may be a range of specific goals compatible with the general ground and the oppositionists may disagree among themselves about which of these specific goals is the best or the most prudent to pursue. For example, when a promotional policy bars the advancement of women and/or minority-group members, a new policy might allow for "token," "merit," or "affirmative action" promotions of those against whom discrimination is directed.

There are many determinants of goal selection. For example, how radically the goal departs from the organization's current modus operandi is often a function of the perceived resources of the opposition group, such as its morale, connections, and bargaining skills. Further, the goals may be influenced by prevailing policies in comparable organizations and may change in the course of the opposition as actions disclose new information, close off options, and open up new alternatives. Finally, the choice of goals may become subordinate to the opposition's strategy through considerations of prudence or the presence of ungrounded motives, such as revenge or the effort to maintain solidarity or avoid dismissal. Oppositions often adapt "satisficing" strategies in which they ask for more than they need or expect so that they can bargain down to their actual goal, which itself only becomes clarified in the bargaining process. The indeterminacy of goal selection is related to the unstructured and unprogrammed nature of bureaucratic opposition. Clarity about goals is, for the most part, a luxury of those who are confident that they have the means to achieve those goals and can count on a consensus about their desirability.

Most generally, the goals of a bureaucratic opposition are either to stop norm violations by having the violator dismissed or reformed, and/or to change a policy in whole or in part. The goals of changing the personnel and of changing the structure are not mutually exclusive. Other things being equal, if there is a choice about which of these two goals to select, then altering personnel will be preferred. The organization is not structurally damaged by personnel changes, so by concentrating on the removal or reform of incumbents the oppositionists can better maintain their loyalty to the organization itself. Attempts to alter policy are more costly. Serpico first went after the removal of several corrupt cops, but then realized that corruption was an unwritten policy of the New York City Police Department. He altered his goal to changing the structure of the Department, to eliminating ineffective, and immoral policy, and met with strong resistance and reprisals. The Watergate investigators also sought "to determined which of the President's men were responsible. The paradoxical conclusion was 'all the President's men'." (3)

Once a goal is set, even provisionally, the general plans for achieving it need to be developed and put into effect. These general plans or strategies fall into two major classes, based on whether they primarily involve giving information about perceived abuses to authorities, outside agencies, or news media, or involve taking direct action against the abuses, such as harassment, filing suit, or disrupting the routine of work. The informing strategy is an attempt to exercise power indirectly by pursuading someone else, usually someone with administrative or legal authority, to rectify the perceived abuse. Direct action, of course, involves the commitment to participate in the power struggle oneself. However, most forms of direct action also require the final action to be taken by those in authority.

For many reasons the informing strategy is the most prevalent used in bureaucratic oppositions. Perhaps the most important reason for this is that it does not appear to be political, it does not seem to commit one to a conflict. The informer often makes the naive assumption discussed above, that if those in positions of responsibility knew that something was amiss they would be grateful for the knowledge and promptly go about setting things right. Informing, then, reminds one of children tattling to their parents about their sibling's misdeeds. The informer can, at least for a while, keep up the pretense that the administrative ideal is honored by the authorities, that there is a normative consensus. As Alvin Gouldner noted, human beings tend to associate goodness with power. (4)

A second reason for the popularity of informing is that it appears to be less costly than direct action, because it relies upon others who have authority to do the "dirty work" of effecting change. Informing appears to leave the decision in the hands of the authority, and, thus, it does not seem to be rebellious. Informers break with business as usual only by violating the chain of command, not by challenging the principle of command itself. They are often not aware, at least consciously, that the authorities tend to associate the chain of command with the principle of command. The informing strategy also seems to be less costly than direct action, because typical instances of direct action, such as work stoppages, may be grounds for dismissal from the organization, while complaints generally are not. Again, the oppositionists are frequently aware that authorities, who are embarrassed, discredited, or compromised by revelations of misconduct, can find excuses for bringing reprisals against dissenters. Informing, then, is as much a political strategy as any other and, of course, many oppositionists understand this from the outset.

Just as the goals of actual oppositions are often multiple and may change over time, strategies are various and mutable. If informing fails, one may continue to inform to higher levels within the organization or to other agencies with authority, or engage in some form of direct action. Disagreement within the opposition group, or merely lack of coordination among its members, may generate the trial of different strategies or tactics simultaneously. In contrast to more structured conflicts such as wars, going in more than one direction at the same time may benefit the opposition because the dissenters are not engaged in a zero-sum game. In particular, informing, despite its risks, does not necessarily consume much in the way of resources. The choice of strategy, however, is not necessarily based on calculations of instrumental rationality. Participants in oppositions usually lack knowledge of the full range of their alternatives and of the consequences of following the options of which they are aware. The use of an "economic" metaphor in this discussion merely serves to indicate that choices are not made randomly and that there is more or less a logic at work which takes costs into account and seeks to minimize risks. If economic rationality were a major concern of oppositionists, however, there would be few bureaucratic oppositions.

INFORMING

There would seem to be nothing easier to do than to provide information about an abuse. However, when the informing strategy is undertaken a number of unforeseen problems may arise. It is not sufficient for the oppositionist to stand in the lobby and vocally announce the abuse or to pass out circulars to those who happen by. The proper recipients for the information must be found and they must be willing to listen.

As hierarchies of authority, organizations attempt to restrict and to control communication as well as to secure the performance of other tasks. Orders are handed down from the top through a chain of command and any information passed in the opposite direction is not supposed to break that chain. Employees are expected to report only to their immediate superiors. Oppositions, however, are frequently directed against just those supervisors to whom the dissidents ordinarily report. Immediate subordinates are more likely to become aware of the rule violations of their superior than are officials at the superior's own level or at higher levels. In order to inform, then, the hierarchy must often be breached.

An opposition group which attempted to inform on a supervisor's discriminatory action against the female accountants in his office went one level higher in the chain of command. However, the supervisor's superior "refused to talk to us because we had failed to follow corporate procedures. He pointed out to us that our first point of contact was Mr. V," the discriminatory supervisor. (5)

Rigid adherence to the hierarchy, which makes informing within the organization impossible, is not the only barrier to communicating about abuses. Some counselors in a drug abuse clinic found out that the vice-directors of the agency had been "skimming money from federal funds for their own personal use. ... The scheme was camouflaged nicely, by talented 'book-juggling' by the culprits. Funds, supposedly used for drug purchases, improving 'job-readiness,' and counseling tools were confiscated by the vice-directors." (6) A statement detailing the malfeasance was drawn up by the counselors and given to the director, but no action was taken. The oppositionists soon learned that the director was also dishonest:

> Therefore, we had to make an appointment which finally got through, to enlighten the Executive-Director to the present conditions. This was fairly difficult to do, because of his 'isolated position' he kept himself in. Finally, after three weeks of trying to get through we got that appointment, by one day barging in his office and announcing we needed to talk to him. (7)

In this case, the information was appreciated and action was taken.

Informing over the heads of one's immediate superiors can also backfire when they are told about it. A weapons analyst in the U.S. Air Force, physicist Kenneth S. Cook, broke the chain of command in the course of his bureaucratic opposition. His immediate commanding officer informed him that he had a copy of his "confidential" letter to the higher brass.

> What followed was a Kafkaesque nightmare. Cook's top-secret security clearance was summarily removed without explanation. ... Then, before a military medical panel ... he was found mentally and physically incapable of performing further service ... within the government. (8)

Similarly, after his superior held up a report about air charter abuses for more than five weeks, a Federal Aviation Administration employee, P.I. Ryther, went over the official's head to the deputy administrator. When he did not take the report seriously, Ryther tried to contact the administrator of the agency. He did not respond and passed the word that he would not comment on the report. Shortly afterwards Ryther was forced to resign when he was "called on the carpet at a special meeting of his superiors for ignoring proper channels." (9)

Working one's way up the organizational chart, even if gaining access is not a problem, does not always make sense. The official chart may not coincide with the way that power is really distributed. The more that the oppositionists are familiar with the "shadow table" (the actual hierarchy of influence), the better they can target their activities. At one university it is well known that one of the several vice-presidents controls or can control all areas of the administration. Several bureaucratic oppositions which began with informing strategies went directly to him, by-passing chart-relevant deans.

Information may be ignored, used against those proffering it, or used to further the goals of the bureaucratic opposition. Monarchs were known to kill bearers of ill tidings and, while not nearly as severe, administrators rarely welcome the bad news that oppositionists bring. Officials more or less correctly feel that improprieties are their responsibility, because they have formal authority over the situation. Often they were responsible for the hiring, promotion, or good ratings of the rule violator. Anthony Jay, author of The Corporation Man, writes:

... the hardest and most thankless task is to tell the higher managers in the corporation that your immediate boss is no good. In the first place, they appointed him, so you are implicitly criticizing their judgment. In the second place, maintenance of corporate authority demands that they take his word against yours. In the third place, no one much wants to employ the sort of person who is liable to go behind his back to a superior and vilify him, even (or especially) if the person is telling the truth. In the fourth place, your motives are bound to be suspected. (10)

Illustrating Jay's point is an opposition which took action against a supervisor of a research staff who "treated the staff in a belligerent and undignified manner." (11) A complaint was lodged with the office manager, who was the next highest authority in the department. It turned out that the manager "placed greater credence on the reputation of the supervisor than on the complaints of the staff." (12) His only action was to tell the supervisor which employees had complained. "In an effort to discourage and prevent future contacts, he scrutinized the work of those employees who visited the Office Manager. When mistakes were found, no matter how significant, the employees were told that they were fired." (13)

Many oppositionists have considered using the informing strategy but have felt that it was too dangerous to undertake because of the potential for retaliation. A police homicide detective maintains that "speaking out against immoral or perceived unethical conduct of superiors can be a dangerous practice.... When a member becomes known as a 'trouble maker,' a telephone call will precede him to every new assignment warning of his character deficiencies." (14) An FBI agent acknowledges that "agents who wrote letters of protest during Hoover's time could expect, at least, to be transferred to an undesirable office." (15)

Various reasons, including the fear of transfer to distant schools, impelled a bureaucratic opposition group of elementary school teachers to pass information through a third party. The teachers opposed their principal's illegal orders to have them coach students for standardized examinations and, also, upgrade their scores. Instead of reporting to the city's board of education directly, they informed the school's P.T.A. and helped the parents draft letters accusing the principal and calling for his resignation. These letters, which were sent to the members of the board of education and the superintendent of schools, did not reveal the identities of the teachers. The opposition group achieved its goal through an informing strategy involving minimal riask. (16)

The tactical issues of how to inform are multidimensional. Is the information to be proffered in person or by mail? In either case, is it to be transmitted by each of the individuals in the opposition separately or is it to be delivered collectively? Available examples show the use of many tactics and it is difficult to generalize about which are the most effective. Physical accessibility, a sense of one's communications skills, the degree that the authority intimidates, and the nature of the information are possible influences on which tactic will be employed.

One of the major problems that informants have is gaining credibility.

The numerous derogatory epithets hurled at informers, such as snitch, squealer, fink, and rat, dampen the urge to give information. John Dean, described as "the pariah of Washington, the detested 'bottom-dwelling slug,' the 'well-poisoner,' Nixon's despised 'Heartbreak Kid,'" (17) recalled his decision to tell what he knew about the Watergate break-in: "Now I felt the razor edge between the squealer and the perjurer. I had never felt more squalid." (18) The negative view of the informer also allows the recipient of the information to be suspicious of it and, thus, to be reluctant to act on it. The automatic labeling of an informer as a "troublemaker" shifts the burden from the accused to the accuser, while imputing personal (non-grounded) motives to the oppositionist classifies the information as mere propaganda, nothing to be taken seriously.

Oppositions mounted by only one person are most easily discredited. A group, as long as it is not perceived to be a mob, is believed to be more objective. Credibility is increased not only by having several people inform, but by the "consistency credits" of the oppositionists and their organizational status. The longer that people have been with the organization as "cooperative team members," the more seriously will the charges be considered. Thus, numbers, consistency credits, and level of status are all resources of the oppositional group.

When some nurses mounted a bureaucratic opposition against an incompetent nursing director, their information was ignored. However, the hospital administrator regarded the same statements with considerably more gravity when some physicians joined the opposition. (19) The effect of the composition of the opposition group on its success indicates that an informing strategy is not independent of considerations of power.

Credibility is also influenced by the evidence used to support the charges. The pervasive legalistic mentality, probably stronger in public than in private bureaucracies, gives "hard" evidence, such as memoranda, disinterested observers, bookkeeping records, or tape recordings, more weight than unsupported recall or hearsay. Some abuses are easier than others to document with evidence convincing to the legalistic mind. Because the bureaucratic opposition depends for its success on the administration acting on its information to eliminate the abuse, the evidence, ceteris paribus, must be compelling enough to overcome inertia. It is very difficult to obtain such convincing evidence, for example, to demonstrate the incompetence of administrators. There is usually no physical object to examine, and if declines in output or morale are cited they can be attributed to factors other than the manager.

Circumstantial evidence and the testimony of subordinates are often insufficient to impel action, especially if the administrators fear legal suits or reactions from the Civil Service Commission or unions. Thus, one informing tactic, as was indicated above, is to inform on an easily demonstrable abuse rather than on the abuse on which the oppositionist's commitment is grounded. For example, the failure of a straight informing tactic on an incompetent supervisor led the frustrated opposition group to take advantage of a situation which would normally have been ignored. "In an emotional outburst the Supervisor insulted a female staff member with the use of sexist and racist slurs." At this stage of the opposition the group was aware that "there was (only) one provision in the company policy for the removal of an employee at the supervisory level - the use of profanity and abusive language to subordinates. (The group) united behind the insulted employee and encouraged her to register a 'formal grievance' with the office manager, who had ignored the oppositionists' previous complaints. (20) A member of the group recalled the efficacy of altering the public ground: "The Staff was now basing its opposition movement on a clear-cut issue of company policy .... " (21) and anticipated the supervisor's removal. The evidence for the new ground was easy to gather and was credible to the administration.

Informing on sexual harrassment is particularly difficult because in serious cases there probably will not be witnesses and there is still a widespread belief that women are seducers "asking for" advances made by males. One woman who was harassed stated: "As in rape cases, the woman is often held responsible for encouraging animal urges in her male co-workers. Almost always, the woman loses." (22) A young girl working as a housecleaner for an older man told her residential counselor that "she wouldn't go back because he grabbed her breast and tried to kiss her." The counselor reports that "my pain and anger intensified when one of our male counselors said, 'She's probably just fantasizing.'" (23) Although there are now many statutes against sexual harassment, the problem still remains one of establishing proof. A lawyer advised women to use a method "that is perfectly legal - that is, to unobtrusively wire one's self for sound by carrying a hidden tape recorder." (24)

Although the lawyer's advice is perhaps farfetched in most cases of harassment, tape recordings have been successfully used to provide indisputable evidence against corrupt police. The lone oppositionist, Detective Ellis, "was outfitted with a tape recorder which he wore beneath his clothing." (25) Ellis feigned interest in joining the activities of taking money from prostitutes, pimps, and drug dealers, and in keeping some of the money confiscated in drug arrests.

In many cases, evidence of abuse is obtainable in incriminating memoranda and other documents. At times these are easily accessible, especially when the violators are unaware of the impropriety of their actions or do not believe that they would be prosecuted for such offenses. However, when they are cognizant of their culpability, they will carefully protect access to potentially damaging material. The prospects of obtaining documentary evidence are increased by bringing individuals who have access to it into the opposition. Such evidence is also more easily secured if the informants can act anonymously and conceal their intentions.

An example of anonymous informing was the effort of one or more employees of the American Medical Association to change some of the organization's illegal and unethical practices by transmitting "dozens of confidential letters, memoranda, and other documents from AMA files ... " (26) to the press. The informant's anonymity allowed continued access to the embarrassing material. Humorously dubbed "Sore Throat" by the higher officials of the AMA, the oppositionist has caused them to hire a private security firm to plug the leaks. Several staff members have been given lie detector tests. (27) Had Sore Throat's intentions and identity been known, the material would surely have not been available to him.

Informing strategy requires convincing evidence and the tactics used to obtain it may include stealth. The directors of a hospital were not impressed by the argument that a doctor made accusing a fellow surgeon literally of killing a number of patients. They took no action against Dr. X. Dr. Harris, the accuser, then obtained more credible evidence than his previous testimony about a pattern to the deaths that were linked with Dr. X. He " ... obtained a master key from a nurse and, alone in the hospital's dressing room, opened locker number 4, assigned to Dr. X. The locker 'was a mess with items strewn about,' Harris testified. 'The thing that struck me were these empty vials of tubocurarine (a trade name for purified curare) and this loaded syringe. That was enough for me. I closed the locker and shuddered.'" (28) "Astounded by the discovery," that is, armed with more solid evidence, the directors finally took action.

Informing strategy in oppositions directed against policies is, ceteris paribus, more difficult than in those aimed at rule violators, if only because of limited accessibility to needed evidence. In an article about managerial strategies, Paul Goodman and Donald Van Houten contend that "limited access to financial and production data plays an ... important role in maintaining the corporate status quo." (29) They conclude, pessimistically, that those "who wish to challenge managerial decisions on rational grounds may thus have inadequate data from which to plead their case." (30)

In order to boost the prospects of the success of an informing strategy, the oppositionist or opposition group may marshal a number of tactics. Among the possible tactics is the use of rhetoric in the disclosure. Rhetorical skill, the power to persuade, is unevenly distributed and may or may not be used self-consciously by the opposition. Particularly when there is resistance against a policy, the dissenters must present arguments and not merely factual evidence. The policy may be shown to be "irrational" because it leads to a loss of efficiency in reaching the organization's goal or because it actually subverts the attainment of this goal. Discriminatory policies are fought by dramatic "demonstration" that members of a group are competent to perform relevant tasks. If the policy contradicts some moral norm the argument may involve what rhetoricians call appeals to authority, invoking the Church, for example. Arguments may be geared to arouse emotions, such as sympathy or prejudice. Appeals to the awesome power of the herd ("Everyone else is doing it") are often useful. Finally, one may appeal to fear, which is more than mere rhetoric. It is the threat of calling on other resources and, as such, borders on direct action.

There is a paucity of data with regard to the rhetoric used by bureaucratic oppositionists. The comparable challenge groups, social movements and revolutionary cadres, use rhetoric too, but theirs is made public as "ideology." When a bureaucratic opposition uses rhetorical arguments the appeals are often created without self-conscious awareness and are hidden from public view. It would be interesting to compare the rhetorical devices used within organizations to those used on a wider public. One might expect the appeal to reason to be more frequent in bureaucratic oppositions than elsewhere because of the specialized content of the issues and the limited number of people involved.

In the use of persuasion, arguments are judged to be strong only within a specified context. The art requires sensitivity to the situation and to the personalities involved. One may play on the honor of the firm or the sympathies of the administrator; appeals may be couched in the "patois" of the organization. One of the more effective of the several tactics used by members of a bureaucratic opposition in a law office, who tried to change a trivial but annoying policy, was to write a memo to one of the partners. In it was explained "the illegality of withholding funds involuntarily"; that is, the memo was couched in the legalese common to their work. (31)

Another tactic used by those without authority to accompany an informing strategy is what may best be described as harassment. This tactic involves repetitive informing, either by the same person or others. It persuades not by reason but by continual annoyance. When the harassing tactic is effective, the administrator, in exasperation, corrects the grounded abuse because his or her inertia has been made too painful. Children, another group of people with no authority and few sources of power, quickly learn this tactic to obtain privileges and goods initially denied to them. Parents are known, much to the delight of manufacturers and advertisers, to cave in to repeated wails of "Buy me, buy me." The housewife, traditionally pictured in a situation not dissimilar to the child's, supposedly resorts to the same tactic - in this case called nagging - to get what she wants.

A special kind of informing with the organization is contacting the board of directors or board of trustees. Appealing to this body differs in several ways from merely going up the organizational chart to a higher-level executive. Most obviously, the office is occupied by several persons, not a single incumbent. More significant is the ambiguous position of the board members who are both insiders and outsiders. They have the highest authority within the organization, appointing those who are charged with the administration of day-to-day affairs within the broad policy guidelines outlined by the board. But they occupy their office, both physically and functionally, very rarely; they are not full-time employees of the organization, but are more like absentee owners. They pursue other occupations, if they are employed. Because of their status as partial outsiders, the act of informing is perceived by them to be a somewhat disloyal. However, the board is the first logical recipient of complaints against the higher administrative officer of any organization. Typically, bureaucratic oppositions whose goal is to oust incumbent presidents go to the board.

Several accounts of bureaucratic oppositions against college presidents have been written up in the news media. Nora Ephron has extensively described two of them in remarkable detail. (32) In an Esquire article ironically entitled "The Bennington Affair," the bureaucratic opposition to remove Bennington College President Gail Parker is analyzed. The climax of the case was the faculty's reporting to the trustees that they had no confidence in her ability as President. Grounding their opposition on Parker's incompetence, the faculty recounted incidents of "poor judgment, tactless-ness, lack of follow-through." (33) They also mentioned Parker's well-known affair with an outspoken faculty member. Ephron hints broadly that many faculty members were not committed to the opposition's grounds. Their motives varied. One professor, who was a major impetus to and coordinator of the opposition, had been acting president the year before Parker was appointed and was thought to have been disappointed that he was not chosen for the permanent position.

Parker antagonized the faculty in various ways and had few consistency credits left. For example, at the customary fall presidential address she read a long section from The Groves of Academe, a novel by Mary McCarthy.

> The section concerned a faculty meeting at McCarthy's Jocelyn College, where the same people got up and said the same things year after year, and nothing happened. To this day Gail Parker cannot understand why the faculty found the reading condescending and offensive; she thought the section was terribly funny - and it is, of course, which is not the point. The Bennington faculty resembled Jocelyn's almost too perfectly." (34)

It was not surprising that when Parker went against tradition to announce sweeping new policy changes without the approval or even consultation of the faculty, the bureaucratic opposition began in earnest. Not only did this precipitating act dishonor them, but the new guidelines were a direct threat. Parker's report called for a reduction in both the number of faculty positions and the percentage of tenured slots. (35) In the Bennington tradition, the president is viewed as a leader rather than an administrator. Thus, the charge of incompetency which led to the vote of no-confidence by the faculty was taken seriously by the Board of Trustees. Parker and her husband, the vice-president, were forced to resign.

At Boston University a bureaucratic opposition to oust its president met with no success at all. John Silber is an abrasive and uncompromising person, and was known to be so by the search committee that selected him as president. They thought, at the time of selection, that he was just who the university needed. The incidents that created the nucleus opposition group of deans involved Silber's handling of the budget. "The deans had turned their budgets in months before, when the budgets were due, and Silber had sent the budgets back to be revised. They turned them in again and Silber had sent them back again" without comment. (36) They resented having to cut back continually, especially when Silber had allocated large chunks of money to support pet projects. Some of the deans discussed strategy. One said that he might resign and was told by another that it was "a futile gesture ... because no one would care if the deans resigned." (37) Within a week two-thirds of the deans agreed to call for Silber's resignation. After word of this was "leaked" to the press "the faculty joined the deans, and at a full Faculty Senate they voted 377 for resignation, 117 against, with 12 abstentions." (38)

The grounds of the bureaucratic opposition to the president concerned his "financial malfeasance." Among other things, he was charged with obtaining interest-free loans, having the university build a private tennis court, and paying for his Beacon Street apartment-hideaway. It is doubtful that these incidents would have raised many eyebrows had they been committed by some other president, one who was not as outspoken and abrasive as Silber. The administrators and faculty composing the opposition mainly wanted Silber removed from office because he had continually dishonored them, but they did not consider this ground to be strong enough. The Board's response to the information about Silber's malfeasance was to have a member confront the president privately, over drinks. Silber deftly "explained away" each charge to the satisfaction of his somewhat inebriated prosecutor. He then mounted a campaign to have statements supporting him sent to the trustees by major politicians and educators. When he formally faced the full Board, many of the trustees arrived thinking that he "was just wonderful." (39) Silber "toughed out" the confrontation and "defended himself brilliantly." (40) Several years have passed since the opposition was mounted and John Silber, whose salary is over $80,000 per year, is still President of Boston University. Why one bureaucratic opposition based on informing to the board of trustees failed while another succeeded cannot be determined with exactitude. One may surmise that the contrasting political climates of the two schools, as well as the personality differences of the presidents and board members, helped cause the divergent outcomes.

The informing strategy is generally the first to be chosen because it appears to demand less commitment than direct action and is relatively less costly. The options within the broad informing strategy include alternative recipients of the information and different ways or tactics of presenting it. If the first try at informing is not successful by the opposition's standards, which may alter, the dissenters may switch to direct action or inform elsewhere. If they choose the latter alternative, they have three directions in which they can move: up (to a higher level on the organizational chart), laterally (to some supportive association such as a trade union), or outside (to a controlling agency or the press).

Many of the same considerations relevant to informing to one's superiors are applicable to lateral informing. Employees are involved with one or more groups to which they can supposedly turn for redress of grievances. These groups, such as unions, the Civil Service Commission, or professional associations, are more or less independent of the organizational hierarchy and can contribute various resources to bureaucratic oppositionists. Such groups may also have some authority over the organization in which the employees work, through laws or contractual agreements. In a sense, they can short-circuit bureaucratic oppositions. When one of their members reports an infraction, their representatives go to management to have it corrected. Because they have some independent authority, their relations are best described as negotiations rather than as bureaucratic oppositions as defined in the present discussion. However, getting a union to take one's grievance seriously and act on it often amounts to making a bureaucratic opposition within the union. Making the organization change its policy is beyond the scope of the union's business-as-usual and involves working the political machinery of the union.

It is not uncommon for union officials to assume the view of the upper echelon of the organization being opposed by the employees. (41) A transit worker in a large city attempted to make some minor policy changes in the municipality-owned system. He first spoke with the union president:

He listened attentively to my plans but refused to take an active role
because he was dedicating most of his time to seeking reelection. He
tried to pacify me by ... indicating that the organization was too finely
tuned to permit changes in one part. (42)

In another case, workers at a warehouse loading dock objected to a new
policy of tightened security measures. They first complained to the foreman,
informing him that the new policy placed an undue physical burden on them
and was also insulting.

Not getting any results from the foreman, the workers decided to go to
their union steward, who by that time was well aware of the situation.
(The union said) .. that they thought the security measures were good,
and they felt no need to change them because the employees wanted
it! (43)

In both of these examples, the failure of informing strategies to lateral
groups led to an escalation to direct action against the employing organization.

The difficulty with using unions to correct perceived organizational abuses
is that their major purpose lies elsewhere. The membership, particularly in
the United States, is interested in decent wage contracts and fringe benefits,
such as medical insurance and paid vacations. Resolving grievances that are
not clear-cut and explicit in the contract is generally beyond the union's self-
imposed scope, and policy disputes are beyond its purview altogether. The
union's power ultimately rests on the strike, thus, informing it of an abuse
which it resolves borders on direct action. However, as far as the employee
is concerned, an appeal to the union is an informing strategy. Ralph Nader
and his associates conclude that

In theory the union may, through the collective bargaining process,
demand both substantive rights to protest work that threatens the
public and procedural devices for a fair hearing when those rights are
asserted. In practice this potential has been neglected. (44)

Unlike bureaucratic organizations, unions have, at least on paper, the
political machinery with which those without formal authority may make
input. Electoral practices and other democratic mechanisms, however, are
often window dressing concealing entrenched oligarchy. The classic study of
union democracy done by Lipset et al. worked from the premise that such
democracy was the exception, not the rule. They attempted to explain how it
is possible for a democratic union to occur rather than why it does not.
Oppositions within unions rarely use informing tactics alone because it is
usually the top echelon that is being fought; informing within the union is
useless. Also, because of the political structure, dissidence is expected to be
worked out through majority opinion as expressed in union elections.
Democracy is more of a sham in some unions than in others. A Teamsters'
member made a proposal at a union convention to slash President Fitz-
simmons' salary. He was beaten by several sergeants-at-arms; "the beating

left his face swollen and purple." Another member charged that "tactics such as adjourning Teamsters' meetings when dissidents try to speak or holding meetings at hours when many union employees cannot attend are common...." (45) In effect, unions which are strongly authoritarian, despite democratic camouflage, are significant for the present study because they are similar to bureaucratic organizations.

Other lateral groups have less power than unions. Employed professionals can inform to their professional association which often can or will do no more, after investigating the charges, than to censure the organization. The association's newsletter will then describe the injustice and put its members on notice to "try" to avoid securing a job at that institution. Among university professors, the tight job market of the 1970s lessened social opprobrium as an effective enforcer of the American Association of University Professors' list of censured colleges and universities. The association's power is mainly the ability to make swipes at an institution's reputation among professionals.

Ernie Fitzgerald, involved in a complex bureaucratic opposition against the cost overruns in the Defense Department, sought help from his professional engineering association when he was dismissed from his job. He asked that the association "investigate the professional and ethical questions involved ...(But) the American Institute of Industrial Engineers suddenly decided it was not a 'professional' society; it was a 'technical' organization. Thus it absolved itself of dealing with ethical questions." (46) The overruns were charged by Lockheed in its work on the C5A cargo plane. Fitzgerald contends that the effectiveness of the AIIE and similar groups is "undermined by their practice of allowing 'sustaining' or 'corporate' members. Large military contractors are contributing members of his own society. ... "(47)

A second type of lateral group is directly incorporated into the bureaucracy. Organizations such as the United States Armed Services have built-in units to redress grievances of those without authority. The Inspector General's Office has been in existence since 1813, and similar agencies are found in the armies of many nations. It is formally independent of any other channels of command. A campus Reserve Officers Training Corps (ROTC) instructor enthusiastically told me that while the suggestions which emerge from the Inspector General's investigations are called recommendations, they are ordinarily received as commands. My general skepticism was nourished by cases of bureaucratic oppositions within the army whose members did not deem it worthwhile to use this Office.

In a United States Artillery installation in Germany a group of young college-educated enlistees found their sergeant to be inordinately abusive. His excessive drilling, overly rigid inspections, unfair distribution of passes, and misuse of recreational funds were intolerable to them. There was no concerted action until "for some minor infraction the sergeant pulled the passes of the entire unit for the whole weekend. While having lunch in the mess hall later that day the unit booed the sergeant as he passed by the window. It was this spontaneous action that precipitated the formation of the opposition group." (48) At a meeting that evening they discussed various courses of action and specifically rejected the use of the Inspector General, believing it to be ineffective. They decided upon an informing strategy. The unofficial leader proposed that they write up a list of their grievances and give it to the commanding officer. Eighteen of the 20 men in the unit signed it. The leader requested the signatures, indicating that he felt that there was "safety in numbers." However, they failed to present the list because the sergeant's permission was needed to do so. Rather than change to direct action or attempt to inform to the Inspector General or to some agency ouside of the army, they used some ingenuity to get to the Commanding Officer (C.O.). The leader gained access on the pretext of "personal problems" and delivered the list. The C.O. was shocked by the list and despite the sergeant's threats ("I'll get you for this") most of the injustices were eventually eliminated. (49)

William M. Evan, in an analysis of the Army's Inspector General Department, gives substance to suspicions about the ability of the I.G. to reduce the need for bureaucratic oppositions. He begins by suggesting that "the I.G. complaint procedure may seem to involve an organizational anomaly in granting all army personnel a legal right to lodge complaints directly with I.G. officers, for it thus sanctions the circumventing of the chain of command." (50) Evan indicates that the chain of command is rarely circumvented in practice, and he supplies various structural reasons to account for the observation. Of greatest importance is the fact that the I.G. personnel are recruited from line officers who, after a brief stint, return to the line. Thus, the officer serving in the I.G. has been socialized "to see the value of the chain of command."

> Upon transfer to the I.G. he learns of the opposing principle of direct and horizontal communication. Since he is destined soon to return to his duties as a line officer, he is not likely to repudiate the principle of the chain of command, much less become committed to the function of the I.G. complaint system. (51)

Also, the officer's transfer to the I.G. is usually viewed as down-grading. Evan concludes that investigators would "prefer that army personnel take up complaints with their immediate superiors ... , and (have) a tendency to view them as being largely unjustified." (52) And although a soldier has the right to lodge a complaint with the I.G., line officers "may be inclined to view such action by subordinates as virtually disloyal conduct." (53) Substantiating Evan's analysis is the narrow call a Staff Sergeant in the Air Force had in using the Inspector General's office. Sergeant Hayden filed a complaint against a superior officer, charging him with conduct unbecoming an officer. An officer of the Inspector General conducted a two-week inquiry and not only confirmed the charges but found further detrimental information against the accused major: " ... petty theft, drinking on duty, and calling the Air Force Secretary a meddling fool and an idiot." (54) The Inspector General asked Hayden to drop the charges and when Hayden refused he was ordered to the mental health clinic for evaluation. There, too, he was asked to drop charges. His refusal led to his transfer into the psychiatric facility at another base, Lackland. Fortunately for Hayden, the doctors at Lackland discharged him with a "clean bill of health" after two weeks of examinations.

Further corroboration of the I.G.'s ineffectiveness is the emergence of unofficial complaint systems. Rather than "suffer in silence," go through the I.G. office, or participate in a bureaucratic opposition, army personnel may bring grievances to the chaplain or to the Mental Hygiene Consultation Service, both of which act unofficially on complaints. (55) Whichever of these three groups are used, the issues involved in informing, particularly achieving credibility and having the abuse perceived as a serious one that should be eliminated, still obtain.

Internally created groups, such as the Inspector General's Office and company unions, are only as effective as their top echelon allows them to be. Corporate malfeasance, on the whole, and rule violation by those in ultimate authority are abuses outside the official jurisdictions of ombundsman-style offices. The types of abuses which they are prepared to take seriously and the scope of the recommendations they are prepared to make are influenced by the climate of each particular bureaucracy. Whether such offices are used or by-passed by employees is a function of their perceived effectiveness. Because they allow their employees to "blow off steam" as they inform, they may function more as "pressure escape valves" than as mechanisms to correct abuses. As such they are rather functional to maintaining the status quo and, thus, it is understandable that bureaucracies have created them.

Ombundsman offices within bureaucracies correspond closely to those created by various levels of government to give their citizens redress of grievances against official agencies. More specifically, they resemble the executive ombundsman found in many American cities and counties more than the classical ombundsman developed in Scandinavia. The latter is an officer of Parliament who investigates citizens' complaints about unfair treatment by governmental departments and who recommends a remedy if a complaint is deemed just. The office was begun in Sweden and Finland and was adopted by Denmark in 1955. Since then Norway and New Zealand, among others, have adopted it. (56)

> The executive ombundsman differs from his classical cousin in that the former is dependent upon the chief executive and serves at his pleasure, while a classical ombundsman, once appointed, serves for a fixed term at least formally independent of the appointing agency. (57)

The lack of independence of the executive ombundsman tends to interfere with the task of redressing grievances, whether the executive is a mayor or a corporation president. (58) It is interesting to note that those governments which have institutionalized the classical ombundsman may be termed the most progressive; they are the best exemplars of the welfare state. They represent, also, Max Weber's fears of a rationalized world - the Crystal Palace where politics has been replaced by administration. The ombundsman provides a small measure of politics in a system that considers politics to be an anachronism. Because the ombundsman offices are ultimately controlled by the administration within bureaucracies, policies and rule violations that are in the administration's interests cannot be opposed by them. Thus, the offices serve a rather limited function in correcting abuses.

A second alternative to informing to one's superiors within the organization, which may supplement or substitute for appeal to a lateral organization, is informing to a governmental agency or to the general public through the news media. "Whistle blowing" may be undertaken after other informing or direct-action strategies have failed or it may be the first resort of oppositionists. When an organization is systemically corrupt it is neither prudent nor effective to inform within it.

The rationale for whistle blowing is that the interests of the public are generally harmed by organizational abuses that are illegal, that violate widespread moral norms, or that breed inefficiency. Both public and private sector organizations are, in some sense, responsible to the public. The consumer, the taxpayer, the citizen, and the patient, among others, are all recipients of the effects of organizations and can be appealed to by the whistle blower. Most often, of course, public outrage at organizational abuses is not very great. (59) Regulatory agencies, which are often staffed by personnel on loan from the organizations that they monitor, also cannot be relied upon to act against reported abuses. Nonetheless, if the oppositionists cannot trust the higher levels of their own organization, they may have nowhere else to go but to the public, or its official representatives in the executive or legislative branches of government, or to independent regulatory authorities.

Although going outside the organization to the public seems to be merely a logical progression in the attempt to make changes in an organization by those without the authority to do so, it is not perceived to be continuous with other strategies. Dissent is interpreted as disorganization and making internal dissent public is viewed as a direct attack on an organization, a treasonous act. Even those outside the organization may deem the whistle blower a traitor: "Martin Luther seems to be about the only figure of note to make much headway with public opinion after doing an inside job on a corrupt organization." (60)

Organizations can be usefully conceived of as miniatures of society.

> They have a hierarchy of status and of roles, a system of myths and values, and a catalogue of expected behaviors. ... (They) meet many of the most basic needs of their members and expect in return loyalty and conformity. (61)

Americans who protested against the Vietnam war were told directly by bumper stickers and indirectly by police actions, "America - Love it or Leave it." Those who have felt the response to whistle blowing are familiar with this kind of sentiment: "the principle is 'your organization, love it or leave it.'" (62) The self-image of organizations as self-contained polities leads administrators to view governmental agencies as foreign powers. Organizations are usually willing to submit voluntarily to governmental authority only when it suits their interests to do so. Otherwise they must be coerced in some way. Bureaucratic oppositionists who call upon the power of Congress, for example, are seen in the same light as the Spanish Republicans viewed Franco's use of German fighter planes or, better yet, as anti-Communists view Soviet support of revolutionary groups in Western democracies or non-Marxist dictatorships.

In the past decade there has been a spate of whistle blowing activities. Several books have been written on the phenomenon itself and conferences have been organized around the theme. (63) It is the form of bureaucratic opposition that is most widely known because gaining public awareness is its central strategy. Whistle blowing, especially when it is the first tactic used in an opposition, is more likely to be done by one person rather than by a group. Perhaps this is partially explained by the extreme risk, including opprobrium, of such action. Going beyond narrow self-interest may be possible in crowds, but opposition groups tend to discuss alternatives "rationally," including the possible reprisals that might be taken against them. Heroic stances are easier to take when others are not around to remind one of the consequences of an action.

Even its supporters recognize that whistle blowing is a strategy that supports a basically conservative position. Informing in general is not designed to change but rather to restore. The information proffered demonstrates that what "is" is not what was "supposed to be." It is designed to provoke outrage - the organization is shown to be exceeding the bounds of authority and/or decency. The bounds, secured by social values, are upheld by the whistle blower, or at least they are espoused in public, whatever other motives may be involved.

A classic example of the whistle blower's temperament is found in Christopher Pyle's opposition against the United States Army's practice of civilian surveillance. In two articles, one published in January and a follow-up in July 1970 in The Washington Monthly, Pyle described in some detail the surveillance apparatus used by the Army and its development after 1967. He also argued vigorously that the Army's activities were unconstitutional. The grounds of this opposition were provisions of the United States Constitution, while the strategy was to make it public that the U.S. Army was violating the fundamental law. The effectiveness of an informing strategy rests upon the commitment of those who have the authority to uphold a standard to enforce it. If the authorities are neither indignant nor enraged about transgressions they will not be moved to take action merely because of the oppositionist's information. Pyle's disclosure did not fall on deaf ears. It was picked up by the American Civil Liberties Union and the press. Senator Sam Ervin, Chairman of the Constitutional Rights Subcommittee, was particularly disturbed and instituted hearings on the case in February 1971. The Senate's power over the Army is related not so much to substantive legislation as to the disbursement of military funding. The armed services are concerned for their budgets. A few weeks after the start of Ervin's hearings the Assistant Secretary of Defense revealed Defense Department regulations that prohibited military involvement in civilian affairs, promised that these regulations would be followed, and indicated that much of the irregularly collected information had been destroyed. (64)

The problems that face all bureaucratic oppositionists who attempt an informing strategy, deciding upon and gaining access to those who should receive the information, and presenting credible evidence to them, are also confronted by the whistle blower. One of the major decisions involves the choice among the alternatives of going to the "authorities," contacting a referee group, or bringing the case to the attention of the general public. (65)

The bases for the selection of one or more of these possibilities are rather complex. Potential whistle blowers may not be aware of all of the agencies that might have an interest in their information. And even if all of the possible recipients of the revelations are known, the oppositionists might believe that most of them would not be sympathetic, that they have been "captured" by the organization they regulate.

With regard to personal security, particularly to future employment, blowing the whistle to a governmental agency is usually less costly than presenting the information to the general public. Not only is more confidential informing viewed as a less treasonous act, but there are often built-in protections for the oppositionist. For example, it is a violation of federal law to retaliate against someone who testifies before a congressional committee. Whether or not potential whistle blowers are aware of the different risks involved in different strategies is not easy to assess. The option selected is usually related to the ground of the opposition. If the abuse is a clear-cut violation of an enforced statute and a remedy is obvious, informing to the appropriate governmental agency is the reasonable alternative.

The selection of the recipient may also be made in terms of the non-grounded aims of the opposition. Even if the whistle blowers are all committed to the grounds and sincerely seek to remove the abuse, their commitment may still be accompanied by a desire for vengeance. Durkheim's distinction between two types of sanctions for rule violations, retributive and restorative, is useful here. (66) The first type of sanction corresponds to criminal statutes and, according to Durkheim, is prevalent in premodern groups characterized by strong we-feelings based on the similarity of each individual to the others. Restorative sanctions, in contrast, predominate in modern societies which have a complex division of labor. People are aware of one another as functionaries who may not resemble them, but upon whom they depend.

The hypothesis here is that those who seek vengeance do not as closely identify themselves with their occupational roles as do those who seek only the elimination of the abuse. Whistle blowing to the general public is a more punitive measure than bringing information to a referee group or to a government agency, especially if the information is not made public. Informing to the public holds the organization up to scorn. Threatening the organization's "good will," lowering the public's opinion of it, is painful to those who identify with that organization. Further, a tarnished public image may lead to fewer customers, lower work effectiveness, or reduced funding by a constituent-pressured Congress. A certain amount of vengeance will be accomplished if some arm of the government calls those who are responsible for the abuse on the carpet. However, other things being equal, more vengeance can be had by going to the general public.

Once the initial choice is made about where to blow the whistle, the problem of obtaining access and of gaining credibility still remains. The approach to a congressional committee or a government regulatory agency is much like the political insurgent's appeal for international support. And as Mostafa Rejai indicates, there is typically a counterappeal by the incumbents.

This taking of countermeasures for international aid is usually easier for the incumbents, since they are in formal control of the political and diplomatic apparatus of the country and since they are likely to have a variety of international contacts. (67)

In like fashion, the heads of the organizations employing the oppositionists, because of their official legitimacy, political ties, access to lawyers and sometimes to large funds, have a greater opportunity to debunk the claims of the oppositionists before governmental agencies than their adversaries have to discredit them. The organization's records are often accepted as valid and even blunt and unsupported denials by officers are greeted as effective rebuttals to the oppositionists. Discussing the problems of labor union members who have attempted informing strategies against the myriad abuses of union officials, Burton Hall remarks:

...the rank-and-file union member who appeals to the Secretary (of Labor) against the union leaders feels that he is appealing to the ally of his enemy to protect him against his enemy.... Yet the law bars union members from complaining of stolen union elections to any court or agency other than this very friend of the officials he is complaining about. (68)

Regulatory agencies were not set up to handle complaints from the employees of the organizations that they monitor. Their inspiration, when it does not emanate from the regulated themselves, comes from other government agencies, legislative bodies, or consumers. The regulatory bodies frequently do not carry out their public charges effectively. For example, the Food and Drug Administration was barraged with complaints from both consumers and physicians about the baneful effects of feminine deodorant sprays, but no investigation was made of the charges. Finally, the Federal Trade Commission, in checking out the truth of the advertisements for this product, advised the Food and Drug Administration (FDA) to investigate. Unable to subpoena records, the FDA took the word of the manufacturers, delaying their own research on the issue. (69) Confidence in the effectiveness of such "watchdog" agencies is further shaken by the existence of bureaucratic oppositions within them.

One such opposition occurred in the Department of Health, Education, and Welfare. It illustrates the difficulties involved in using such agencies to aid bureaucratic oppositions, because it demonstrates the effect of politics on the will to enforce the law. The Office for Civil Rights, authorized by Title VI of the Civil Rights Act of 1964, was responsible for seeing that schools, universities, hospitals, nursing homes, and welfare agencies which received HEW subsidies did not engage in discriminatory practices. OCR Director, Leon Panetta, was rather effective in accomplishing his duties, much to the chagrin of the new Nixon administration. In February 1970 he was dismissed and his staff understood this action as "simply the climax of a series of attacks by the Administration on 'the program'...." (70) Their bureaucratic opposition, planned in numerous strategy discussions, was to protest against the policy to the White House, since the President was the ultimate chief of their bureaucracy. Their opposition, grounded in charges of ineffectiveness, used strategies other than informing, such as several high-level resignations and a letter signed by almost 2,000 HEW employees.

Another case of a bureaucratic opposition within a government agency involved the microbiologist J. Anthony Morris. For a decade he had been at the National Institutes of Health, involved in experiments on the long-term effects of flu vaccine. The response to his internal memo that questioned the benefits of flu vaccine was the removal of his staff, his experimental animals, and laboratory, and the blockage by his superiors of the publication of his scientific articles. (71) Helped by one of Ralph Nader's "raiders," his statement detailing the irregularities of the NIH flu vaccine program set off investigations by Senator Abraham Ribicoff and the General Accounting Office. Morris' whistle blowing to the government resulted in HEW Secretary Elliot Richardson transferring him to the Food and Drug Administration to continue his flu research. No punitive or remedial action was taken against or within NIH. In 1976 Morris publicly criticized the swine flu program. He had tested the live vaccine in mice and found that it was potentially carcinogenic. Further, he claimed that it might trigger various neurological illnesses, including Guillan-Barre Syndrome. Morris turned out to be correct and the Federal government has agreed to pay "reparations" to those who suffered from vaccine-related disorders. The Commissioner of the Food and Drug Administration, however, fired Morris for "insubordination." Thus, even well-grounded bureaucratic oppositions are not always successful. Morris upheld the organization's official functions, to protect health, and presented information that showed the organization's policies were detrimental to health. Rather than being rewarded for his efforts, he was punished.

Congressional subcommittee hearings seem to provide would-be whistle blowers with once-in-a-lifetime opportunities to gain a receptive audience for their revelations. In the early 1960s Senator Kefauver headed a committee investigating the drug industry. A medical director at E.R. Squibb and Sons, Dr. A. Dale Console, testified on the ways in which drug sales were increased by the exploitation of physicians. (72) Although Dr. Console was apparently committed to a bureaucratic opposition on moral grounds, he gave a psychological explanation for his action: "I had compromised to the point where my back was against a wall and I had to choose between resigning myself to total capitulation or resigning.... " (73) "The invitation to testify before the Kefauver Committee offered him the platform he sought." (74)

Similarly, an employee of the Internal Revenue Service from 1948 to 1971 came forward (the religious metaphor is appropriate) at the Senate subcommittee hearings on the Internal Revenue Service conducted by Senator Montoya. Stanley Prescott described policies which resulted in the "abusive treatment of the taxpayer" and the "violation of taxpayers' rights." (75) Prescott's grounds for opposition were the immorality and the ineffectiveness of policy. He stated that "the overseer at each level must find among his subordinates at least one 'weak' employee and 'help' him into unemployment or a nervous breakdown." (76)

With seizures and the threat of seizures hanging over taxpayers' heads, the fear to which IRS employees are subjected is thus passed on to the taxpayer, which is the whole intention of the program anyway. (77)

The Senate Watergate Committee allowed numerous White House bureaucrats to blow the whistle. It is doubtful that Alexander Butterfield, a major aide of John Haldeman, would have informed on his bosses had he not been called upon to testify. It was Butterfield who revealed the existence of Nixon's taping system, which made the President's "stonewalling" technique ineffective. He did not regret giving the testimony, however. 'I was a loyal troop,' he explains. 'But my mother also raised me to be an honest troop, and I told the truth. No other way.'" (78) It is difficult to determine whether Watergate was an externally provoked opposition or a true bureaucratic opposition as the phenomenon is defined here. The identity of Deep Throat would make it easier to classify the affair.

Whether or not congressional hearings are held to advance political careers, as a journalist with conservative leanings claims, (79) they do seem to encourage whistle blowers. In 1975 Nicholas von Hoffman remarked that "these days you can't walk in a door in the Capitol without coming upon somebody recounting to a raised row of legislators some awful business of official betrayal and ignominy. The tales they tell in these hearing rooms of government murders, burglaries, and pornographic pictures are incontestably icky...." (80)

One such tale-teller was ex-Marine Hardy. As a paid informant for the FBI he was not as fully embedded in the Bureau's hierarchy as an agent. He told Otis Pike's congressional committee on intelligence how the FBI paid him to lead a raid on a draft board. (81) Although Hardy considered the policies that he had executed to be immoral, it is not likely that he would have initiated a bureaucratic opposition had the Pike hearings not occurred. They provided a whistle-blowing forum where he could give the detailed information about the abuses without much fear of retaliation and could also clear his troubled conscience: "I only hope and pray that by coming here today, I can right some of the wrong that was committed." (82) It seems that the spate of congressional hearings that started with the Watergate investigations has abated. Perhaps future election years will generate their reemergence, encouraging both political careers among members of Congress and the testimony of whistle blowers.

Another arm of government, the courts, can be used by those without authority to correct abuses in their places of employment. The ground of the bureaucratic opposition must be some organizational rule violation or policy that breaks a public law. Unless the information that one has would interest a district attorney or federal prosecutor, who would then base a case on it, going to court is a costly and time-consuming undertaking.

The successful use of a public prosecutor is illustrated by a bureaucratic opposition mounted by a lone employee of the Good Humor Corporation, the ice cream producer. The identity of the informer is not known, but he or she told the Brooklyn District Attorney's office that the ice cream was knowingly marketed with an illegally high bacteria count. Furthermore, the company was keeping " ... two sets of quality control records: a false one to show state inspectors and an elaborately coded secret set containing true bacteria counts for the company's own use. The secret books showed coliform counts on some batches of ice cream 200 times as high as the law allows." (83) The District Attorney investigated and subpoenaed company records. Although several thousand documents had been destroyed, enough evidence remained for the oppositionist to sit back as a grand jury handed up a 244-count indictment. (84) The press-dubbed "Ice-cream gate" was a successful bureaucratic opposition in which the legal system acted on information and allowed the employee to maintain anonymity.

The costliness of informing in court by suing the organization results from the need to have professional help and adequate evidence. There are a number of possible sources of assistance, such as the American Civil Liberties Union, that have helped bureaucratic oppositionists use the courts to check organizational abuses. Access to the courts, then, often requires access to interest groups that can provide resources. Also, there are governmental agencies that are empowered to press law suits. For example, the Office of Civil Rights within the Department of Health, Education, and Welfare can bring a case before an administrative court if there is evidence of discriminatory practices. But administrative courts, like the Federal judiciary, have the ability to construe rules more or less strictly. Thus, despite "watertight" evidence, there is no guarantee of success.

Use of the courts is made especially difficult for those who cannot obtain legal assistance. Mike LaVelle, a columnist who champions blue-collar interests, reports:

I have run into a few cases where a union member has asked me if I knew of a good labor lawyer and then added, "I can't seem to find one. As soon as they find out that my beef is against a union they won't have anything to do with me."(85)

A further difficulty for those wanting to inform to the courts or to their union is that "the by-laws of some unions allow them to fine a member or expel him if a worker files any legal action against the union." (86)

Relative to informing against one's organization to the government, bringing charges to a private referee group is, in general, easier but less effective. Such groups vary widely in their areas of concern, modes of action, and sources of support. Among them are the Anti-Defamation League, Consumers Union, Underwriters Laboratories, Sierra Club, and Common Cause. Some are independent of the groups and organizations that they monitor (for example, the Consumers Union), while others are supported by these organizations (for example, the Better Business Bureau). Referee groups are distinguished here from lateral groups because the latter are formed by employees while the former are either created by the organizations themselves or by some constituency.

Referee groups may sometimes take legal action against abuses where there are codes of good practice, as in the numerous "self-regulated" industries. For example, New York Stock Exchange members may "discipline member firms for defrauding customers or for failing to maintain adequate supplies of working capital." (87) However, most referee groups utilize the methods of persuasion, which may vary from rational arguments to threats of public exposure. They may also serve as conduits to access for oppositionists to more directly powerful agencies such as courts and legislative committees. When the National Institutes of Health took Dr. Morris' laboratory facilities away from him after he disagreed with their position on flu vaccines, he was helped to present his case to Congress by the public interest organization, Common Cause, and by Ralph Nader's group. (88)

Other referee groups, such as the Consumers Union, act by directly exposing abuses to the public. Whether or not they have their own publishing vehicle, the press, which accepts their information as highly credible, will help the exposure. These referee groups appear to be effective in aiding bureaucratic oppositions against the production of dangerous goods. Although it is possible to debate the potential danger of a product, it is far easier to reach consensus that people should not be physically harmed by their purchases and to "prove" that an item is unsafe, than to demonstrate such intangibles as dishonor, injustice, or even inefficiency.

Perhaps because of the actual or perceived difficulties in obtaining effective action by informing to referee groups, governmental agencies, courts, or Congress, many bureaucratic oppositionists bring their information directly to the general public. Some take this route because the nature of the abuse is complex or not specifically covered by law, although it is judged to be an offense to public morality. There are other reasons for going public, such as the oppositionist's wish to remain anonymous or to damage the reputation of the organization.

Many oppositionists who inform to the public do so only after failures of other options. An example is Karen Silkwood's bureaucratic opposition against the plutonium plant in which she was employed. The Kerr-McGee Cimarron River facility makes plutonium pellets for nuclear power plants. Ms. Silkwood was highly critical of the plant's health and safety procedures. She had gone to her union, the Oil, Chemical, and Atomic Workers Union, "claiming definite instances of company sloppiness." (89) The OCAW had little influence with management but helped Silkwood to present her case to the Atomic Energy Commission. As a result of the Commission's inaction, she compiled careful documentation of safety lapses and contamination and was on her way to blow the whistle. She had her evidence in a brown manila folder and a notebook which friends had seen in her hands just before she left for her appointment with a reporter from The New York Times. (90) She never met the reporter and was found dead in her wrecked car. There was good reason to believe that she had been murdered, particularly because the evidence she had with her was never found. (91)

The AEC finally did complete its investigations. It found that only a few of the numerous allegations referred to possible violations of the Commission's standards, but admitted that many others "had substance or partial substance." (92) The AEC did not put an end to the dangerous situation, however, and wary environmental groups conclude that the AEC is an ineffective regulator because it "needed the fuel rods and thus had a clear interest in keeping Kerr-McGee's plant in operation." (93) Karen Silkwood never had the opportunity to give a statement to the press, but informing to the media was clearly a logical recourse for her after the failure of her informing strategy.

Informing to the general public is somewhat different from going to various superiors within the organization, to a lateral group such as a union, or to some arm of government. When following the latter courses, those to whom one presents the information have the authority to act to eliminate the abuse or at least have the power to put pressure on those who do have such authority. The public is several steps removed from the ability to change the objectionable actions. Instrumentally, citizens can pressure politicians to take action through individual contacts, organized lobbies, or the expression of opinion, among other means. However, immediate remedies are usually ruled out by this informing strategy. Informing the general public is similar to bringing information to Congress which may become more widely known through press coverage, because the consequences may overflow the goals of the opposition. Sometimes bureaucratic oppositionists acknowledge the possible repercussions and use the informing strategy merely as a tactic within an overall strategy of direct action.

Taking one's case to the public is more complicated than playing the town crier with prefacing shouts of "Hear ye, Hear ye!" Communication in a mass society is mediated by complex organizations. Thus, informing to the public-at-large requires the use of the news media, where the usual set of informing problems, such as gaining access and establishing credibility, are encountered. However, because newspapers and television newscasts are business enterprises, there are additional considerations. Frequently the media employ criteria that are not relevant to "the public interest," such as what will boost profits or maintain business power in general. Even if the oppositionist's information is not suppressed, it may be reported in such a way as to raise doubts about the credibility of its source. Despite obstacles, however, many bureaucratic oppositions succeed in placing their facts before the public.

There are a few media outlets that are very cooperative in publishing the information of bureaucratic oppositionists. The magazine Washington Monthly and Jack Anderson's syndicated column have been used by many whistle blowers to present their cases. Both are modern-day exponents of the muckraking philosophy. Its notable representatives, Upton Sinclair, Ida Tarbell, and Lincoln Steffens, did their work prior to World War I. In newspapers and books muckrakers exposed unseemly, corrupt, and dangerous practices of politicians and corporations. Their work was characterized by an attitude of "throw-the-rascals-outism." (94) As professional journalists, the muckrakers were not employed by those who they exposed. In a sense, a person who blows the whistle is "the muckraker from within." (95)

A bureaucratic opposition mounted by staff members against Senator Thomas Dodd used the columns of Drew Pearson and Jack Anderson to reach the public. Relying on the rest of the Senate to take action against the abuses which grounded their opposition would probably have been fruitless. There were two major and interconnected grounds for the opposition: Dodd had been syphoning off hundreds of thousands of dollars from campaign contributions for private use, and had accepted funds from those whose vested interests he supported on the Senate floor. The opposition consisted of Dodd's administrative assistant, James Boyd, and an office secretary, Marjorie Carpenter. Peters and Branch's description of the bureaucratic opposition indicates that Boyd, anguished by the corruption, had intended merely to "leave quietly and loyally." (96) A 1964 election campaign report filed by Dodd for the State of Connecticut was so fradulent that the decision was made to expose the malfeasance, but only after the Senator had dishonored his assistant. Boyd recalled: "The campaign diversion in 1964 was bad but it took Dodd's malevolence to make his actions real - not abstract. I felt small and like I was being toyed with for the first time since I was in the Marine Corps." (97)

Actions that dishonor members of the opposition group are not unusual catalysts for the emergence of dissent. Several accounts similar to Boyd's can be found in the statements of other oppositionists. The rage felt at insults is often sufficient to overcome the fears of the risks involved or, as in Boyd's case, the appeal of a good position. The reaction to dishonor, however, does not rule out a strong commitment to the grounds of the opposition. Boyd and Carpenter failed to take action, despite their initial decision, for six months. They have candidly revealed their thoughts during this period:

We kept wondering 'Who are we to take him on?' And there was always a fear of looking naive - of summoning up a burst of moralism and then having everyone laugh and say that's just the way things are done. (98)

But Boyd and Carpenter did finally act, giving their information to Jack Anderson "who encouraged them with his muckraker's fervent argument that the public had a right to know if there was evidence of foul deeds behind Dodd's senatorial pomp." (99) Twenty-three columns were devoted to their information over a period of several months. Pressured by an informed public, the Senate voted to censure Dodd. However, support for the judgment that difficulties are involved in using the press is provided by the fact that the first two of the columns were suppressed by The Washington Post. Only edited versions of the others were printed after Drew Pearson exerted pressure. (100)

Informing to the press is probably easier since Woodward and Bernstein's capitalization of Watergate, with the aid of the indispensable Deep Throat. Investigative journalism has become the rage. Newsmen are willing to use "tips" from insiders to expose wrongdoing. Giving data to the press is often a way of getting political officials to take the complaints which are simultaneously revealed to them seriously. Such whistle blowing is frequently a costly escalation of informing and is often tried after initial failure with intraorganizational personnel. A typical illustration is the opposition mounted by two nurses at the Shiprock Indian Health Service Hospital, located on a Navajo reservation in New Mexico. (101) The nurses complained about filth and poor patient care, protesting for three months through the hospital's chain of command. They then sent a letter describing the conditions to President Ford, which was also published in a local newspaper. They were admonished and within a month were fired for "continued disruption of the work force and conduct unbecoming an Indian Health Service Employee." (102) The charge against them was, in essence, "washing dirty linen in public," a deed sure to displease any administrator.

Frank Serpico's opposition mirrors the nurse's plight, although it was far more protracted and dangerous. He had gone up the line of command within the New York City Police Department in an effort to combat the corrupt practices that abounded. He soon learned that accepting payoffs was not a rule violation committed by a random few, but was an unofficial policy, condoned by the highest echelons. He enlisted the aid of the Internal Security Division of the Department, but was soon disheartened by their inaction. He was unable to reach the Mayor, only getting as far as one of his aides. (103) Serpico's friend, David Durk, had earlier suggested going to the press:

> Durk had a contact on The New York Times, and they would go to him and blow everything wide open. ... He reasoned, it was highly unlikely that The Times would act simply on the say-so of two cops at their level, even though Durk was a detective. ... Serpico had another thought. Suppose a superior officer, a full inspector, a Paul Delise, accompanied him to The Times and confirmed what he had to say about corruption in the department and the system which allowed it to flourish? That, maybe, would make a difference. (104)

Serpico was aware that he had a problem of gaining credibility for his information with the press. At first Delise refused to join the opposition, pleading: "I have a wife and kids, and I just bought a house and there's a mortgage on it, and if I had to leave the department I don't know what other field I could go into. ..." (105)   But Delise was finally persuaded to accompany Serpico and Durk to the Times contact. Serpico was correct that he needed an upper-level police officer to support his information. The Times journalist, Burnham, indicated that if "Delise hadn't been there, nothing would have happened." (106) Burnham's editor gave him the go ahead to write up a three-part series about police misconduct with Serpico's revelations interspersed throughout. When the story finally appeared in print it set off a spate of similar ones in the competing daily newspapers, and on radio and television news programs. The Mayor appointed an independent investigatory Commission headed by a lawyer, Whitman Knapp. Several suits were brought against the Commission by the police. One of them declared that the investigation might result in "great expense, harassment and inconvenience to policemen." (107)

Serpico gave testimony in both the closed and open phases of the Knapp Commission's investigation. Unlike other witnesses who concentrated on the misdeeds of specific persons and who testified because they were granted immunity from prosecution, Serpico repeatedly stressed the policies of the department that allowed corruption to flourish and, more important, that did not permit honest police work.   Despite the publicity generated by the investigation, only a few individuals were charged with offenses and they received minor administrative punishments.   The overall policy which encouraged corrupt and ineffective activities remained intact.

Serpico's opposition shows some of the problems of the informing strategy in general.   Because he did not have documentary evidence, as did the anonymous "Sore Throat" who opposed the American Medical Association, Serpico needed to supplement his word with the testimony of a higher official. Serpico also could not control the direction that the response to his revelations took. While he had realized painfully that the entire system was corrupt, the ensuing investigation concentrated on specific misdeeds.

A two-man bureaucratic opposition against Southwest Bell Telephone Company was able to get incriminating information into the newspapers despite the lack of "hard evidence." The method used to gain credibility, however, was costly. One of the two oppositionists, T.O. Gravitt, a chief executive for the phone company in Texas, committed suicide and left a detailed death note. In it he stated that the company was making political payoffs, doing illegal wiretapping, and using questionable bookkeeping methods to secure telephone rate increases. (108) According to Gravitt's widow and James Ashley, the other member of the opposition who was general commercial manager for Southwest Bell's San Antonio office, the suicide was a direct result of the company's attempt to squash the bureaucratic opposition. "Ashley claims that when Bell learned that he and Gravitt were planning to expose such practices, the company started investigating their private lives." (109) Gravitt's family and James Ashley won a slander suit against Southwestern Bell for three million dollars, but in light of the events, one may question whether the opposition was successful. (110)

Another way of disseminating information to the public about organizational abuse is to publish a book. Like the other means of informing, this tactic has difficulties. The information has to be both substantial enough to fill at least part of a book and capable of arousing public interest. If the latter requirement is not met the manuscript will probably not be published by a commercial press and, therefore, will not be distributed widely or reviewed in magazines and newspapers. "Vanity" publishing is not usually effective for oppositionists, although it is possible for a privately published work to be picked up by a commercial press if it has some success. Other difficulties with publishing arise if the organization to be exposed has enough clout to discourage publishers from printing the damaging information. For example, several former agents have tried to publish books exposing the illegal, ineffective, and immoral policies of the Central Intelligence Agency. Philip Agee had to have his book, Inside the Company: CIA Diary, published in London by Penguin Books. At least three American publishing houses, Straight Arrow, Simon and Schuster, and Warner Paperback had "been dissuaded from publishing it by the prospect of interminable legal hassling and expense." (111) Having to write the book after leaving the CIA was also difficult for Agee. He wrote it "abroad while bugged and hounded, he claims, by Company agents." (112) Once the book was in print there was a concerted effort to discredit the author. Agee was called a Communist agent, a traitor, a fool, a drunk, and a womanizer. (113)

Victor Marchetti, a former high-ranking CIA official who has co-authored a book exposing the Agency, has also been harrassed in his efforts to make evidence public. Portions of this book, CIA and the Cult of Intelligence, written with John Marks, a former State Department official, had been censored prior to its publication. The CIA also obtained a permanent injunction, upheld by the Supreme Court, which prohibits Marchetti from "writing or saying anything, 'fact, fiction, or otherwise' about intelligence without prior approval of the Central Intelligence Agency." (114) The Agency even tried, though unsuccessfully, to block the publication of the book by attempting to discredit Marchetti's character with the publisher. Another exposure of the CIA, John Stockwell's book In Search of Enemies, was published secretly by W.W. Norton. Only six people within the company knew about the project. (115)

It is instructive to compare the bureaucratic oppositions of Victor Marchetti and Philip Agee. Both chose to publish books as the way to inform the public and they exposed similar types of organizational abuses. Both resigned from their positions before writing their respective books. Yet the goals of their oppositions differed. Marchetti, who had a high rank within the Agency, hoped that the information he provided would "win public support for a comprehensive review of the CIA in the congressional arena." (116) That is, Marchetti wished to curb the abuses, to reform the Agency. In contrast, Agee's case described the limit of bureaucratic oppositions: his goal being the abolition of the CIA. (117) Agee does not believe that significant reforms of the Agency are possible and, so, he aims at the bureaucratic analogy to revolution in the polity.

Publishing a book about organizational abuses has several drawbacks that tend to make it a less effective tactic than other variations on the informing theme. The author often becomes a celebrity while the book's message is relegated to a secondary importance. Philip Agee complained: "people seem more interested in me and my potential trajectory than in what I can say about the Central Intelligence Agency." (118) Also, while the public expects the press to check on the facts and to serve as an authenticator of them, the same expectation does not apply to book publishers. Finally, blowing the whistle through publishing a book allows the oppositionist to gain financially and, therefore, casts doubt upon the veracity of the story.

The advantages of exposing abuses through a book include the whistle blower's control over the context in which the information is presented. He or she can both analyze the causes of the problems identified and offer proposals for change. The book can also serve as a public confession, since many bureaucratic oppositionists have participated in the abuses that they later expose or try to eliminate. For example, Victor Marchetti comments on Philip Agee's expose:

I am a Catholic. I understand what Phil was trying to do in his book. This was his sincere act of contrition and complete confession that every Catholic has to make before he dies so that he at least has a chance to go to heaven without a mortal sin on his soul. (119)

Most bureaucratic oppositions which inform to the general public are undertaken by people who are no longer employed in the target organization. Usually the whistleblowers resign, but if they do not, as soon as their "treasonous" act is known they are usually fired promptly. In those bureaucracies where the employees have some protection, such as those covered by civil service regulations, paychecks may still arrive, but the executive or professional informer will not be allowed to do any meaningful work. When informing outside of the organization is done by those who were never employed by it, the phenomenon is no longer classified as bureaucratic opposition, because different principles of action and consequences apply. The outside informer, for example, cannot be deemed a traitor. Also, external oppositions often do not have as much access to confidential information as do informers from within.

Bureaucratic oppositions using an informing strategy focus all of their attention on the grounds of the opposition. Their method is to gain access to those who are empowered to act to remedy the abuse and to give them the "facts." The underlying assumption of informing is: "If they only knew, boy, would they be angry!" When this assumption is contradicted, the oppositionists either believe that the person who heard them is an exception and proceed to look for a more appreciative ear, or they become disillusioned and give up, or they explore the possibilities for direct action.

While the informing strategy is often based on the belief that "the facts speak for themselves," direct action is governed by the premise that the "facts" must be supported by power. If the facts do speak for themselves then the number and status of opposition-group members should make no difference for success. Ideally, an informing strategy works like the feedback given by a thermostat to a furnace or a gyroscope to a steering mechanism, maintaining a steady state or an equilibrium. The information should be sufficient to correct the "error." Of course, the ideal of the informing strategy is nearly never actualized. Because of the risks involved in undertaking a bureaucratic opposition, which are often most severe when one goes outside the organization, and the general lack of rewards if the opposition is successful, whistle blowers tend to be highly committed to the grounds they publicly announce. They are the most idealistic of oppositionists, whether in terms of the public goals of an institution, the laws of the state, or the precepts of a moral system. They are also the firmest believers in the efficacy of the "facts."

Informing strategy is most applicable to getting rid of incumbents who have violated important organizational rules, especially if these rules are backed by wider cultural standards. Oppositions against organizational policies that run counter to strongly held norms of the larger society may be able to inform effectively to authorities outside of the organization or to the general public. Bureaucratic oppositions grounded in abuses other than these two are less likely to employ informing effectively and often find direct action to be more expedient.

DIRECT ACTION

The informing strategy presupposes that the recipients of revelations about abuses share a formal if not a personal commitment to the norms or values grounding the opposition. Frequently, however, oppositionists find that such a consensus does not exist, or they are aware of dissensus from the outset. When the authorities do not subscribe, at least officially, to the public goals of the opposition, the dissenters must develop strategies that exert influence or power more directly. The use of persuasion to alter the value commitments of authorities is a possible option, but it does not seem to be an effective one, because higher administrators are not known to be favorable to having their goals changed by subordinates. Debate over value commitments is an effective mechanism of change only where political participation is legitimate, and it is not in bureaucracies. Thus, oppositionists who do not inform or who go beyond merely providing information usually attempt either to rectify the abusive situation by themselves or to get the authorities to make the desired changes despite their disagreement. In both of these cases the oppositionists usually must admit to themselves and to others that they are engaged in a political conflict.

The distinction between informing tactics and more direct exercises of power or influence is not sharp and in many concrete cases the two shade off into one another. Each type of strategy can be used subordinately to the other in a variety of circumstances, but in the most frequent cases a basic informing strategy is bolstered by other tactics. Some of these instances have already been described. For example, when the Bennington faculty informed on the college's president to the board of trustees "dozens of impassioned faculty galleys arrived at the offices and homes of the trustees." (120) The oppositionists assumed, correctly or not, that merely describing the grounds, citing the president's incompetence, and expressing their lack of confidence in her leadership ability was insufficient. To get the board to fire Parker they felt that they had to spell out the detrimental consequences of her behavior in a dramatic way. Although the faculty members believed that they shared a normative community with the trustees, they augmented their presentation of facts with arguments and with demonstrations of mass indignation. In this case the power of rhetorical persuasion was used within an informing strategy to convince authorities that the conditions grounding the opposition were seriously discrepant with common values.

Another dramatic way of highlighting the seriousness of an abuse is the recruitment of those with relatively high status in the organization to inform with the original opposition group. This tactic is analogous to the rhetorician's argument from authority. A group of nurses attempted to remove the director of nursing services from office on the grounds of incompetence by allying themselves "with a group of militant anti-administration doctors ... " who presented their complaints to the hospital's board of directors. (121) This tactic was unsuccessful, but it was easily converted into a direct-action strategy that will be discussed below.

The presentation of arguments may be accompanied or replaced by various actions with persuasive aims. Administrators who do not share an oppositionist's judgment about a certain policy may reexamine their stand when the employee resigns in protest, particularly if it is done publicly and supplemented with whistle blowing. Resignation adds greatly to credibility, in the same way as did the suicide of the telephone executive cited above.

A bureaucratic opposition was mounted by three middle-management engineers who were employed in the nuclear energy division of General Electric Corporation. They did not believe that the radiation-containment safety devices in nuclear plants provided adequate protection. Their superiors did not seem to be concerned about the functioning of the system and denied ever having heard the engineers' complaints. (122) The engineers decided that because of the safety hazards nuclear reactors should not be produced. Thus, they opposed the goal of the division in which they were employed on moral grounds. The authority to which they appealed was the general public, since they assumed that the corporation was not interested in abolishing one of its major divisions. They called a press conference to announce 'their resignations, and to assert that the nuclear power plants now in operation in the United States "are plagued by design defects and operating problems to an extent that poses a major safety dilemma for the nation." (123)

Their action was directed towards changing the values of citizens who might pressure state or national governments to regulate nuclear plants out of existence. The effect of their resignation was assessed by one journalist, in a front-page story, in the following terms:

> It was like a shot heard 'round the nuclear energy world, signalling what could become a national reappraisal of the growing dependence on nuclear power in the United States. (124)

A direct attempt to exploit the drama of a situation to change a practice was made by some legal secretaries in Chicago. They wanted to eliminate the office policy that required them to prepare coffee for their bosses. (125) One of the secretaries in the office protested this policy verbally and was promptly fired. The others then came to the office dressed in waitress' uniforms. (126) Their action is reminiscent of the tactics of the Yippies, who threw money onto the floor of the New York Stock Exchange where brokers ran over one another to retrieve the bills. Both events dramatized the values of the opposed practices for those involved in them. By holding up a mirror, distorted to be sure, it was hoped to shame the opponent into abandoning the practice. It is difficult to assess the efficacy of the secretarial opposition because the local news media publicized it. Had the secretaries intended to use a whistle-blowing tactic they could not have chosen better. Access to television newscasts is made easier when the visual element is emphasized and even more so when people look slightly ridiculous. The fired secretary was rehired and the policy was changed.

When the women's movement began denouncing the treatment of females as sex objects, but before anyone had thought to struggle against such dishonor by legal or administrative means, a secretary told me about a political tactic used in a bureaucratic opposition against a boss who made lewd remarks about her and her co-worker's bodies. He was particularly intrigued by breasts, but would observe and comment on other parts of the body as well. The two women began to feel more and more demeaned, but were sure that if they complained to him or to any other male they would be met with derision. After some months of frustration they hit upon a tactic which proved effective. Whenever they looked at their boss they stared directly and continuously at his crotch. He became flustered almost immediately but it took him some time to make the connection between their stares and his own behavior towards them. Nothing was said but he no longer closely observed or commented on their bodies. One suspects that his standard of appropriate behavior toward women was changed by the secretarial guerilla theater and not by a change in his appreciation of their anatomy.

Some bureaucratic oppositions use informing as a tactic to accomplish a hidden goal. Particularly when the aim is to remove a superior from office, or to restrict his or her power, the dissenters may try to build a case by presenting evidence of infractions that do not really concern them. Here informing is neither idealistic nor naive, but instrumental and manipulative. The dissenters rationally choose the information that will be taken most seriously by the authorities, and select the most sympathetic and effective recipients; they exercise political savvy. This tactic is feasible in many oppositions. Subordinates, especially assistants, aides, and secretaries, are often privy to compromising information which they generally help to keep hidden because of their loyalty. Abuses which diminish this loyalty allow the use of confidential data. As in the case of dramatizing tactics, informing with ulterior motives requires some acting ability. One must pretend to some show of outrage over conditions that are not felt to be abusive.

Acting and dissembling are also required when informing itself is disguised under a cover of sociability. It may be effective and diminish risks merely to chat with a superior's boss on a person-to-person basis; thus, a member of the bureaucratic opposition group who has social access to an administrator is a great asset. Showing no sign that one is pleading a case, disparaging remarks, gossip, and insinuations can be dropped which put the abusive superior in a bad light. The more that one is aware of the particular values held by the administrator, the better one can tailor one's "casual" conversation. The grounds to which the oppositionists are committed need never be mentioned. The aim here is to have the superior viewed less favorably, to redefine the situation as viewed by the higher administrator. If the tactic is effective, the targeted superior will no longer be given the benefit of the doubt and otherwise innocuous behavior may be judged to be grounds for dismissal.

The various means of dramatization and the devious uses of informing are embroideries of the basic informing strategy. There is a class of tactics, however, that rely upon verbal expression, but which border on or constitute direct action. As the courts have recognized, speech may incite or harm as well as provide information. In bureaucratic oppositions speech ordinarily becomes direct political action in the form of threats.

The power to threaten a superior with informing others about an abuse is available to all employees who dare to use it. The assumption is that while the superior does not object to the rule violation or disputed policy, at least not strongly enough to take remedial action, he or she acknowledges that higher authorities might be outraged if they were apprised of the situation. In most cases it is probably less risky actually to do the informing than to threaten to do so. The threat gives the superior time to cover tracks, to prepare a case against the oppositionists, or to try to silence them. Threats can evoke cooptation offers, counter threats, or even physical attacks. Karen Silkwood supposedly was murdered when it was found out that she was going to blow the whistle on her employers. (127)

A special variant of the tactic of threatening is the threat to resign. The assumption here, whether made explicitly or merely understood, is that the organization will be adversely affected by the oppositionist's departure. The threat of resignation is meaningful when those issuing it are not readily replaceable, and it has long been viewed as a test of power in the polity. Authorities who give in to such threats are perceived as weakening their control, and according subordinates a veto power over decisions.

The bureaucratic opposition against an incompetent director of nursing services at a suburban hospital, which was mentioned above, escalated its attack to the tactic of threatening resignation after trying numerous means of informing. The group recruited some doctors to give them more authority when they informed. The hospital administration finally acted and removed the director when the doctors issued an ultimatum indicating that they would leave en masse in two weeks if remedial action were not taken. (128) Doctors are not easily replaced and the resignations would have diminished the effectiveness of the hospital greatly.

In an even more successful case the staff (nurses, mental health and social service workers) at a psychiatric hospital opposed the authority structure of the organization on the grounds of ineffective policy. The doctors, who visited the hospital infrequently, had administrative control over the therapy program, and thus, over the staff. The opposition argued that the staff

> ... should be free from outside control so it could develop its own treatment philosophy and experiment with different approaches. It seemed rather obvious that the psychiatrists had become rigid in their approach. They were, in effect, alienating themselves from the unit workers and from their patients while perpetuating their own roles without evaluating their efficiency. (129)

Presentation of their case to the administration did not meet with success, but when the staff threatened a mass resignation, which would have closed the hospital, the authorities reluctantly gave in and changed the structure. (130)

The threat of resignation, however, sometimes backfires. A number of college book travelers opposed their supervisor's unethical sales methods and threatened their mass resignation if the practices were not changed. The sales department made no response to their move. In effect, their bluff had been called and, one by one, the salesmen resigned.

The use of threats as an opposition tactic is always risky because a threat is a direct attack on an adversary, an open acknowledgment of conflict. If the bluff is called and the threat is not carried out, credibility, power, and dignity tend to be lost altogether. The costs of threatening are, at one extreme, dismissal or actual physical harm, and, at the other, a breach of the trust that is necessary to conduct day-to-day business without uncertainty and tension. At the very least, those who threaten show that they no longer uphold the myth of obedience to authority. In contrast, nonverbal political tactics allow the oppositionists to appear to be as loyal as ever - the opposition to a supervisor, for example, can be kept a secret and yet be effective.

Abusive supervisors are particularly appropriate targets for being secretly undermined. A telephone company employee, who was a member of a group that wished to oust a foreman who made disparaging remarks about his subordinates, indicates why and how such a tactic works:

> The job of the foreman is to make sure that the workers are doing their specific task. But most often, the foreman never knows how the workers do their job. All telephone problems are discovered and solved through a computer. The foreman has only been trained about basic

computer "know-how." On the other hand, the workers know how to 'foul up the works' long enough for just a little trouble. The foreman gets called 'on the carpet' every time the computer "goes down" - stops for some unknown reason. Note that this is an effective means of opposition because the foreman does not know enough about the computer to know if he has been deliberately set up or not. He just "looks bad." (131)

The astute participant-observer assesses this tactic:

> ... the workers can oppose without getting reprimanded in any way. It has one drawback however; the workers cannot attend the meetings of the officials when the foreman is being called in. So the workers never know if they are having any success. (132)

In order to overcome their uncertainty and gain quick results, the opposition- ists tried another strategy which resulted in reprisals. What they did not know was that before they had implemented their second strategy the administration had decided to transfer the foreman. The opposition had been successful in making him look incompetent, but its members learned about their effectiveness too late. They underestimated their power, the source of which was their technical expertise.

This tactic is also described by Robert Merton with regard to its use against political appointees or elected officials who are in charge of public bureaucracies: "if the bureaucrats believe that their status is not adequately recognized ... detailed information will be withheld from (the official), leading him to errors for which he is held responsible." (133) Here, too, job expertise is a source of power for the "lower participants." David Mechanic formally states the principle involved:

> Other factors remaining constant, to the extent that a low-ranking participant has important expert knowledge not available to high- ranking participants, he is likely to have power over them. (134)

Making a superior appear to be incompetent need not rely on expertise. Sabotage may be effected by other means. For example, a secretary may insert a compromising sentence into a letter dictated by her boss, who usually signs his correspondence without reading it over. Possibilities for disruption proliferate once the decision to begin hostilities is made.

An alternative tactic to sabotage, which is also aimed primarily against superiors who are perceived to be abusive, is harassment. As was noted earlier, the harassment of employees is often a ground for opposition. Administrators who are blocked from dismissing disliked employees by union or civil service rules frequently attempt to make life at the workplace difficult for them. A government report on whistle blowing notes:

> Informal harassment is a common bureaucratic practice ... often used against whistle blowers because it is difficult to prove and quite often the employee has not done anything technically improper to justify formal action. (135)

Oppositionists do not usually have the authority to create difficulties for their targets legitimately, but they may be able to exercise informal power.

In a small municipal agency a bureaucratic opposition used psychological warfare against an abusive supervisor. She was what may be termed a "power freak," ever eager to display her control by committing injustices and dishonoring her subordinates. After the supervisor had dishonored the individual with the least tenure and the weakest personality in the office, all of the subordinates met to chart their opposition. They believed that the agency's director and his administrative assistant were not concerned with the office and, thus, that informing would be fruitless. They decided to use psychological pressure to try to get the supervisor to resign or at least to be less abusive. They isolated her; "Her attempts to engage in conversation were totally ignored." (136) Each morning the employees greeted one another with exaggerated friendliness but did not even speak to the supervisor. Having no one else in the office with whom to be sociable, the supervisor was effectively ostracized. The tactic itself probably would have been sufficient to get results, but success was speeded when the administrative assistant noticed the situation and inquired about its cause. The staff told him about the problems and shortly afterwards the supervisor was reprimanded and certain functions were removed from her authority.

Ostracism is not the only means by which subordinates can drive their superiors to want to leave a position. Neurotic tendencies can be exacerbated and reinforced to the point at which the target of the opposition does become emotionally incapacitated. When the tactic is successful the superior either quits or is dismissed, but when it is not the oppositionist's situation is probably worse than it had been before.

Pushing an abusive superior over the brink has also been literally attempted and sometimes effected. There are many cases of murder or battery by "disgruntled" employees against supervisors. Most often such incidents are based on perceived dishonor suffered by the subordinate and occur after a reprimand or a dismissal. Battery against the foreman has, in fact, been glorified in country music. Murderers, of course, are not allowed to enjoy the new bureaucratic climate that they have created, unless they can escape detection. A seeming example of the use of murder as a tactic in a bureaucratic opposition took place in a perfume factory in New Jersey. A worker, Robert Mayer, brought suit in a federal court against the company, alleging safety violations. Three months after the suit was thrown out of court he walked into the factory "...and, without a word, shot to death the company president and two plant foremen..." (137) He then killed himself. In this respect murderers resemble the "alumni" whistle blowers who do not seek anonymity and who have no intention or hope of regaining employment in their former organization. Murder and whistle blowing are also similar because most cases mix grounded opposition with emotional intensity.

Forcing a superior to leave the organization through psychological or physical pressure is the only use of power in which bureaucratic oppositionists need not ultimately rely on those with authority to put the desired change into effect. There is, however, another possible tactic against abusive superiors which might preserve the anonymity of the oppositionists. Rather than try to make superiors appear to be incompetent, as did the telephone workers mentioned earlier, the oppositionists might attempt to goad and guide them into actually committing some abuse or violating a rule that is considered to be important by the authorities. Ideally such transgressions would be obvious to the higher levels of administration or the evidence of them strong enough to be presented anonymously. A variation on the same theme, if the situation was not ideal, would be to inform on the artificially induced abuse. In the use of this tactic the rule violation would not serve as the ground to which the oppositionists were committed; their power of cunning would be used to provoke and induce a grounded abuse. It is of interest that in none of the more than one hundred cases of bureaucratic oppositions of which I have accounts has this tactic been deployed. Omniscient narrators did not write the case descriptions and those who might use this kind of tactic may either be ashamed to own up to their deeds and/or be afraid that admission might overturn, even at a later date, the successful opposition.

The various tactics of harassment, psychological pressure, and deception are most effective against abusive personnel, but have little applicability in policy disputes. Policies cannot be changed directly without administrative action, nor can they be altered indirectly by tactics such as goading in which the authorities are not aware that there is an organized opposition. It is possible, however, for subordinates to use "the power of lower participants" to make it plain that the administration's projects will be obstructed.

Many if not most workers have the power that comes from their bending the rules to achieve greater efficiency. Thomas Scheff describes the power that hospital ward attendants have over physicians. (138) The paper work concerning medication is extensive and is the official responsibility of the doctor. The attendants assume some of this work, which allows them influence over decisions made about the patients. If the attendants opposed some policy they could refuse to fill out the numerous forms which are not their responsibility. The tacit threat of such action keeps the physicians from making policy changes that would displease the attendants.

One of the more popular kinds of direct action, the greve du zele ("work by rule"), consists of "slowing down the work flow and paralyzing the functioning of the organization just by observing, to the letter, all the required prescriptions ... " (139) This tactic involves an open attack upon the effectiveness of the organization and requires the participation of a large percentage of the work force. It trades upon the paradox that rule infractions are instrumental to the efficient functioning of the organization.

> (Although many organization theorists have stressed) ... the functional characteristics of rules within an organization, it should be clear that full compliance to all the rules at all times will probably be dysfunctional for the organization. Complete and apathetic compliance may do everything but facilitate achievement of organizational goals. (140)

Work-by-rule is probably a popular tactic because it requires the oppositionists to obey the rules, not to break or circumvent them. Work slowdowns, which result from strict adherence to rules, are often psychologically rewarding to the participants as well as minimal in their risks. Because the action impairs the functioning of the bureaucracy, participants and others, both inside and outside the organization, become aware of the importance of the work they have been doing.

A bureaucratic opposition in the suburban-area marketing department of a major telephone company was grounded in dispute over a policy change. A team of efficiency experts had been brought in and they proceeded to reevaluate jobs, install a new set of procedures, and increase the norms of expected output. One of those affected by the reorganization reported that

> Employees became so caught up in paper work, detailed procedures and seemingly unnecessary reports, many of which were repetitious, that our department began to lose sight of its real purpose, which was the sales and servicing of our markets. (141)

The opposition seemed to be grounded not only in the inefficiency and ineffectiveness of the new policy, but in the judgment that the department had been dishonored, that departmental authority had been usurped by the consultants. The new procedures also resulted in a number of demotions, transfers, and forced retirements. The informant expressed the mood of the dissenters: "Our plea was to have the honor of having our own management team attempting to get rid of bunglers rather than these outsiders." (142)

Their collective action consisted of a work slow down in processing each order and a refusal to put in the overtime needed to clear up the situation. The results were that the number of installation orders dropped sharply and the installers complained. Customers, many of them large businesses, sent in a rash of complaints, some directly to the president's office. Not only did the oppositionists recognize the importance of their jobs, but the tactic was appropriate to the abuse, and therefore psychologically satisfying. They were aggrieved by the imposition of new rules without consultation - "The administration only seems interested in our functioning with mechanical efficiency." (143) Their work-by-rule tactic told the upper echelons, "Well, if you treat us as machines we will behave as machines. Machines will follow all directions explicitly, have no flexibility or discretion, and will not put in any extra effort. We will show you how ineffective machines are!"

A similar opposition in a legal office used, among other tactics, a greve du zele to oppose a minor personnel policy that was thought to be unfair.

> We decided to do everything by the rules. Time cards which affect billing time were fully written out with no abbreviations. All long distance calls were refused unless accepted by an attorney. No Xeroxing was done without an appointment in the Xerox log. Nothing was notarized by secretaries until completely read. Nobody signed their bosses' names to documents no matter how urgent the necessity of sending out the document became. In essence everything the office manual required was done. But this really fouled up the system because of the numerous informal rules which had developed were no longer being followed. (144)

The sense of poetic justice associated with this tactic was obvious and satisfying to the opposition group members: "If the unfair policy was coming from the office manual then we will show you how stupid that manual is by obeying all of its rules to the letter."

The gratification felt by many of those who initiate a greve du zele is underlined by the fact that this technique is used as an end-in-itself. Frequently slaves and others who feel that they cannot successfully make any changes in their conditions engage in continuous work slowdowns. Others call them "lazy" or "stupid" but they and their comrades know that they could work much more rapidly and with greater precision. "Backstage" they exaggeratedly mimic themselves to show that they know that they are purposely "presenting themselves" as having diminished capacity. Their gratification comes from "putting one over" on their masters and the poetic justice of "you treat me as less than human and I will behave accordingly."

Work stoppages are similar to greve du zele because they also require widespread support. Both tactics presuppose that the administration values effectiveness and efficiency enough to make concessions if these goals are threatened. The power exhibited in a work stoppage is the least specialized resource of the "lower participant." Mechanic states, "To the extent that a person is dependent on another, he is potentially subject to the other person's power." (145) The strike, then, depends for its efficacy upon the difficulty of replacing the dissidents. Those with highly specialized skills have greater leverage than those without them who also often have clauses banning wildcat strikes in their employment contracts.

The strike which is initiated and authorized by a union is not a bureaucratic opposition as defined in this study because it is a type of inter-organizational conflict rather than a movement for change from below. The wildcat strike, however, since it is not sanctioned by union authority and may even be a rebellion against it, falls squarely within the bounds of the present discussion. Unionized workers are knowledgable about strikes in general, so it does not take much creativity to suggest a wildcat. The solidarity nurtured for strikes called by the union also serves wildcatters. The tactic requires a strong sense of camaraderie that exceeds any loyalty to the union or, of course, to the employer.

Coal miners are well known for the use of wildcat tactics; their bloody labor history and the dangerous conditions of their everyday work have helped to establish very strong bonds among co-workers. Many Appalachian locals of the United Mine Workers union engaged in unauthorized work stoppages during the summer of 1977. The workers were protesting cutbacks in miners' health benefits. On June 20, 1977, the miners received a letter stating that they would each have to pay 40 per cent of medical costs up to $500. Until then they had enjoyed free medical care, the legacy of John L. Lewis' negotiations. "The next day, scarcely a ton of coal was mined in Eastern Kentucky." (146) The change in policy came about because of the depletion of the medical funds contributed by the owners on the basis of days worked and tonnage mined. The contributions had dropped in part because of previous wildcat strikes.

The national union election had been held less than a week before the change in medical policy was announced and, despite denials of any foreknowledge, re-elected United Mine Workers President Arnold Miller was suspected of complicity by the rank-and-file. The wildcat strike probably hurt him more than it affected the mine owners:

> The longer it lasts, the less leverage Miller will have in national contract talks. Moreover, his authority in the union is rapidly eroding... (147)

The workers, who wished to have their medical benefits restored immediately, were not satisfied with Miller's explanations that they would have to wait for national contract negotiations to open. After the workers refused to go back to work, the union hierarchy dispatched "armed organizers from Pennsylvania to do battle with unruly picketers." The wildcatters broadened their opposition and mounted a recall movement against Miller. The situation was not resolved before the national contract was negotiated, as was evidenced by the great coal strike of 1978 which grew directly out of this bureaucratic opposition.

Wildcat strikes are direct challenges to the authority of the union hierarchy and they are rarely undertaken when the union leadership can marshal effective violence to enforce its control. When single members or small groups oppose a union they cannot strike, but may resign. If they do so they are often vulnerable to reprisals if they attempt to keep working in the same line. For example, an electrical worker attempted to oppose corruption in the Communications Workers of America. When he realized that the abuses could not be cleaned up by his efforts he resigned, not in protest, but because he did not want to support a corrupt union. He was harassed, beaten, and fired. (148)

Work slowdowns and stoppages are highly visible protests that sharply define a conflict situation. They are opposition tactics that are aimed at changing administrative policy and, more rarely, personnel by diminishing organizational effectiveness and efficiency. It is often possible for workers to oppose a policy without bearing the costs of open confrontation by circumventing the rules or ignoring them. Disobedience itself is not necessarily a tactic of bureaucratic opposition. To qualify it must be interpreted as insubordination both by the workers and by the authorities. Executive orders may not be carried out merely because of misunderstanding or inability to comply rather than because of defiance. (149) Robert Presthus observes that "In organizations, people rarely withhold consent. Rather, they evade, procrastinate, 'misunderstand,' 'forget' ... " (150) Such actions are not bureaucratic oppositions because there is no attempt to change the organizational policy.

Self-conscious and conspicuous disobedience of an organizational rule is an oppositional tactic which directly challenges the principle of command. Unmistakable defiance not only may cause inefficiency but also dishonors the authorities. (151) Many administrators tend to believe with Chester I. Barnard that

... the efficiency of an organization is affected by the degree to which individuals assent to orders, denying the authority of an organization communication is a threat to the interests of all individuals who derive a net advantage from their connection with the organization ... (152)

Frequently, open disobedience is succeeded by other tactics because reprisals are taken against some of the participants. These reprisals may be swiftly enacted because authorities usually have the legal or administrative right to retaliate against rule violations without interference by unions or civil service commissions. Thus, broad participation is an important factor for the success of defiance. Reprisals are not easily directed against more than a very small percentage of the work force without damaging efficiency.

The host of tactics open to bureaucratic oppositionists, whether within an informing strategy or direct action, does not assure success. There is no way of estimating what percentage of oppositions achieves their goals of eliminating an abusive administrator or changing a policy. Some movements are defeated swiftly, others may escalate from less costly tactics to more risky ones. Combining two or more tactics may be effective when done either simultaneously or in sequence. Some oppositions do not fulfill their goals but continue to fight nevertheless. A few try to become permanent by formally organizing.

PROD is a group of Teamsters Union members who are opposed to the corruption of the union hierarchy. The group has existed for a number of years and has a research director and a newspaper to enable it to inform on the leadership. (152) Engaging in other tactics such as court suits and informing to the government, PROD is a multifaceted and resourceful opposition group. It can offer some protection against executive retaliation and has finances and manpower that dwarf oppositions within other bureaucracies. Such institutionalized dissent as PROD is the limit of bureaucratic opposition, because it borders on the creation of a new lateral organization with a specialized staff and hierarchy of its own. As Max Weber noted, formal organization means routine. The essence of bureaucratic opposition is to disrupt routine, which is why its tactics are so diverse and the probabilities of their success so difficult to determine.

CHAPTER 4: NOTES

(1) Maurice Duverger, "The Two Faces of Janus," pp. 111-114 in Michael A. Weinstein (ed.) The Political Experience: Readings in Political Science, New York: St. Martin's Press, 1972, p. 113.

(2) Bernard Brodie, "Strategy," International Encyclopedia of the Social Sciences, Vol. 15. New York: Macmillan, 1968, p. 281.

(3) M. David Ermann and Richard J. Lundman, "Deviant Acts by Complex Organizations: Deviance and Social Control at the Organizational Level of Analysis," The Sociological Quarterly 19 (Winter 1978), 56.

(4) Alvin W. Gouldner, The Coming Crisis in Western Sociology, New York: Basic Books, 1970, p. 85.

(5) Student Paper F.J., 1976, p. 4.

(6) Student Paper C.H., 1976, p. 2.

(7) Ibid., p. 4.

(8) Ralph Nader, Peter J. Petkas and Kate Blackwell (eds.) Whistle Blowing: The Report of the Conference on Professional Responsibility. New York: Grossman Publishers, 1972, pp. 169-170.

(9) Ibid., p. 177.

(10) Anthony Jay, The Corporation Man, New York: Pocket Books, 1973, pp. 81-82.

(11) Student Paper L.W., 1976, p. 4.

(12) Ibid., p. 5.

(13) Ibid.

(14) Student Paper J.L., 1978, p. 9.

(15) Student Paper J.F., 1978, p. 6.

(16) Student Paper O.N., 1976.

(17) Sally Quinn, "John Dean: No Tears, Scars," Chicago Sun-Times (October 24, 1976), 4.

(18) Ed Magnuson, "Expedient Truths," Time 108, #17 (October 25, 1976), 83.

(19) Student Paper D.B., 1976.

(20) Student Paper L.W., 1976, p. 8.

(21) Ibid.

(22) "Ms' Gazette News," Ms VII, #1 July 1978 : 86

(23) Ibid.

(24) Ibid., p. 88.

(25) Leslie Maitland, "Story of an East Side Policeman who Turned in Fellow Officers," New York Times (July 3, 1977), 1.

(26) James Pearre, "AMA Sweats Out Case of 'Sore Throat' Telling Its Secrets," Chicago Tribune (August 17, 1975), 10.

(27) Ibid.

(28) "Suspicion Gathers Around 'Dr. X'" Chicago Tribune (January 12, 1976), 18.

(29) Paul Goodman and Donald R. Van Houten, "Managerial Strategies and the Worker: a Marxist Analysis of Bureaucracy," Sociological Quarterly 18 (Winter 1977), 199.

(30) Ibid.

(31) Student Paper D.J.M., 1976, p. 15.

(32) Nora Ephron, "The Bennington Affair," Esquire 86, #3 (September, 1976), 53-58, 142-151 and Nora Ephron, "Academic Gore," Esquire 88, # 3 (September 1977), 76 ff.

(33) Ibid., "The Bennington Affair," p. 150.

(34) Ibid., p. 144.

(35) Ibid., p. 146.

(36) Nora Ephron, "Academic Gore," op. cit., p. 145.

(37) Ibid., p. 146.

(38) Ibid., p. 147.

(39) Ibid., p. 148.

(40) Ibid.

(41) In 1978 22.5 million workers, 24% of the U.S. labor force, belonged to a union. ("Union Muscle Flexes Far Beyond Numbers," U.S. News and World Report (May 1, 1978), 57.

(42) Student Paper C.S., 1976, p. 6.

(43) Student Paper D.A.D., 1976, p. 10.

(44) Ralph Nader et al., op. cit., p. 187.

(45) Patricia Anstett, "Teamster Rebel Leader Launches Reform Campaign," Chicago Sun-Times (September 19, 1977), 66.

(46) Ralph Nader et al., op. cit., p. 52.

(47) Ibid.

(48) Student Paper O.O., 1976.

(49) Ibid.

(50) William M. Evan, "The Inspector General in the U.S. Army," pp. 147-52 in Donald C. Rowat (ed.), The Ombudsman: Citizen's Defender. London: George Allen and Unwin, 1965, p. 148.

(51) Ibid., p. 149.

(52) Ibid.

(53) Ibid.

(54) Jack Anderson, "AF's Soviet-Style Hush Up," Lafayette Journal and Courier (July 13, 1978), A-8.

(55) William M. Evan, op. cit., p. 150.

(56) Donald C. Rowat, "Introduction," The Ombudsman: Citizen's Defender. London: George Allen and Unwin, 1965, pp. 7-10.

(57) Stanley V. Anderson, "Comparing Classic 1 and Executive Ombudsmen," pp. 305-315 in Alan J. Wyner (ed.), Executive Ombudsmen in the United States. Berkeley: University of California Press, 1973, p. 307.

(58) Isidore Silver, "The Corporate Ombudsman," Harvard Business Review 40 (May/June 1967), 77-87.

(59) The reasons why the "public" is not an effective actor lie beyond the scope of this study.   See Durkheim on the decline of the "collective conscience" in modern, organically solitary society (Emile Durkheim, The Division of Labor in Society. Glencoe, Illinois: Free Press, 1947), and the work on the reaction to white-collar crime (Edwin H. Sutherland, White Collar Crime. New York: Holt, Rinehart and Winston, 1961).

(60) Charles Peters and Taylor Branch, Blowing the Whistle: Dissent in the Public Interest. New York: Praeger, 1972, p. 19.

(61) Robert Presthus, The Organizational Society: An Analysis and a Theory. New York: Vintage-Random House, 1962, p. 94-95.

(62) Ralph Nader et al., op. cit., p. 26.

(63) They include Ralph Nader et al., ibid., and Charles Peters and Taylor Branch op. cit.

(64) Charles Peters and Taylor Branch, ibid., p. 74.

(65) For a discussion of referee groups see Harold J. Leavitt, William R. Dill and Henry B. Eyring, "Rulemakers and Referees," pp. 259-77 in M. David Erman and Richard J. Lundman (eds.), Corporate and Governmental Deviance: Problems of Organizational Behavior in Contemporary Society. New York: Oxford University Press, 1978.

(66) Emile Durkheim, op. cit.

(67) Mostafa Rejai, The Strategy of Political Revolution. Garden City: Doubleday, 1973, p. 38.

(68) Burton Hall, "Introduction," pp. 1-8 in Autocracy and Insurgency in Organized Labor. New Brunswick, New Jersey: Transaction Press, 1972, p. 6.

(69) Joseph A. Page, "What the FDA Won't Tell You About FDS," Washington Monthly 5, #1 (March 1973), 19-25.

(70) Peter Gall, "The Culture of Bureaucracy: Mores of Protest," Washington Monthly 2, #4 (June 1970), 75.

(71) Alexander Cockburn and James Ridgeway, "Scientist J. Anthony Morris - He Fought the Flu Shots and the U.S. Fired Him," Long Island Press (Parade Magazine), (March 13, 1977), 20,22.

(72) Ralph Nader et al., op. cit., p. 118.

(73) Ibid, p. 121.

(74) Ibid.

(75) Stanley Prescott, "Why and How IRS Needs Reforming," Freedom XIX (September/October 1974), 3.

(76) Ibid.

(77) Ibid.

(78) "Alexander Butterfield," People Weekly 3, #15 (April 21, 1975), 66.

(79) David C. Martin, "Probes Reveal Frequent Abuse of Nation's Intelligence Agencies," Indianapolis Star (December 14, 1975): 20.

(80) Nicholas von Hoffman, "Witness for the Betrayal," Chicago Tribune (November 25, 1975), section 2, p. 4.

(81) Ibid.

(82) Ibid.

(83) "'Ice Cream Gate'," Time 106, #7 (August 18, 1975), 67.

(84) "Ice Cream Maker Charged," Lafayette Journal and Courier (August 7, 1975), A-2.

(85) Mike LaVelle, "Shielding Workers from their Unions," Chicago Tribune (May 26, 1977), section 3, p. 4.

(86) Ibid.

(87) Harold J. Leavitt et al., op. cit., p. 267.

(88) Alexander Cockburn et al., op. cit., p. 22.

(89) "The Silkwood Mystery," Time 105, #3 (January 20, 1975), 47-48.

(90) B.J. Phillips, "The Case of Karen Silkwood: The Mysterious Death of a Nuclear Plant Worker," Ms III, #10 (April 1975), 66.

(91) Ibid., p. 66, and "The Silkwood Mystery," op. cit., p. 48.

(92) "The Silkwood Mystery," ibid., p. 48.

(93) Ibid.

(94) Charles Peters et al., op. cit., p. 14.

(95) Ibid., p. 4.

(96) Ibid., p. 24.

(97) Ibid., p. 25.

(98) Ibid.

(99) Ibid.

(100) Ibid., p. 26.

(101) "Burocracy Tale: Don't Blow Whistle," Chicago Tribune (May 12, 1975), 12.

(102) Ibid.

(103) Peter Mass, Serpico. New York: Bantam Books, 1973.

(104) Ibid., p. 251.

(105) Ibid., p. 252.

(106) Ibid., p. 253.

(107) Ibid., p. 300.

(108) "Phone Calls and Philandering: Ma Bell's Slip Shows in a San Antonio Courtroom," Time 110, #10 (September 5, 1977), 32.

(109) Ibid.

(110) "Phone Company Loses Suit," Lafayette Journal and Courier (September 13, 1977), 2.

(111) Alexander Cockburn, "Agee's Book (as Yet) Unbanned," Village Voice (June 16, 1975), 43.

(112) James Atwater, "Company Man," Time 106, #5 (August 4, 1975), 62.

(113) Doug Porter and Margaret Van Houten, "CIA as White-Collar Mafia: Marchetti Ungagged," Village Voice (June 16, 1975), 46.

(114) Ibid., p. 43.

(115) Richard R. Lingeman, "Book Ends: Secrets, Secrets," New York Times Book Review Section (May 28, 1978): 27.

(116) Doug Porter et al., op. cit., p. 43.

(117) Ibid.

(118) Philip Agee, "Why I Split the C.I.A. and Spilled the Beans," Esquire 83, #6 (June 1975), 128.

(119) Doug Porter et. al., op. cit., p. 46. Another possible benefit of publishing a book as a whistle-blowing tactic is that it may serve as protection for the author. That is, the authorities may think twice before retaliating against the whistle-blower since the public will now know that such actions are related to the author's attempts to rid the organization of abuse. An example of this, taking place within the polity rather than an

organization, has been noted with respect to Aleksandr Solzhenitsyn. The person who arranged for the translation and publication in the West of his first Gulag book "...did not immediately grasp the nature of Solzhenitsyn's tactics in his struggle against the K.G.B. --to insure the utmost publicity and literary fame in the West as a safeguard against imprisonment. It would seem that this extraordinary man was able from the outset to foresee the tremendous impact his writing would have in the West and calculate that the Soviet authorities would not dare to imprison an author who had become an international celebrity. (Leonard Schapiro, "Trails of a Translator," The New York Times Book Review (August 13, 1978), 13.)

(120) Nora Ephron, "The Bennington Affair," op. cit., p. 148.

(121) Student Paper D.B., 1976, p. 4.

(122) "The San Jose Three," Time 107, #7 (February 16, 1976), 78.

(123) Casey Bukro, "Nuclear Plants: Safety Dispute Mushrooms," Chicago Tribune (February 16, 1976), 1.

(124) Ibid.

(125) The results of a survey of middle and top-level secretaries indicate that over three-fourths of them served coffee to their bosses, and over fifty percent were also responsible for making coffee as well. ("Secretary as Servant is Typical," Chicago Tribune (August 14, 1977), 37.)

(12) Seen on several locally televised news programs in Chicago during February 1977.

(127) B.J. Phillips, op. cit.

(128) Student Paper D.B., 1976.

(129) Student Paper M.S.P., 1976, pp. 3-4.

(130) Ibid., p. 6.

(131) Student Paper B.R., 1976.

(132) Ibid.

(133) Robert K. Merton, "Bureaucratic Structure and Personality," Social Forces 18, #4 (May 1940), 564.

(134) David Mechanic, "Sources of Power of Lower Participants in Complex Organizations," Administrative Science Quarterly 7, #3 (December 1962), 357.

(135) United States Senate Committee on Governmental Affairs, The Whistleblowers: A Report on Federal Employees who Disclose Acts of Governmental Waste, Abuse and Corruption. Washington, D.C.: U.S. Printing Office, February 1978, p. 27.

(136) Student Paper M.H., 1976, p. 9.

(137) Worker Kills Boss, Self," The Purdue Exponent 94, #115 (September 12, 1978), 2.

(138) Thomas J. Scheff, "Control over Policy by Attendants in a Mental Hospital," Journal of Health and Human Behavior 2 (1961), 93-105.

(139) Michel Crozier, The Bureaucratic Phenomenon.   Chicago: University of Chicago Press, 1964.

(140) David Mechanic, op. cit., pp. 362-63.

(141) Student Paper P.W., 1976, p. 2.

(142) Ibid., p. 5.

(143) Ibid., p. 6.

(144) Student Paper D.J.M., 1976, pp. 11-12.

(145) David Mechanic, op. cit., p. 352.

(146) Fred W. Frailey, "Wildcat Strikes: Preview of Turmoil in Coal Fields," U.S. News and World Report 83, #10 (September 5, 1977), 65.

(147) "Coal and the UMW Are Still at Odds," Business Week #2498 (August 29, 1977), 29.

(148) Kenneth Y. Tomlinson, "The Lonely Ordeal of Dale Richardson," Reader's Digest 106 (May, 1975), 124-28.

(149) Chester I. Barnard, The Functions of the Executive. Cambridge: Harvard University Press, 1938, p. 165.

(150) Robert Presthus, op. cit., p. 137.

(151) As greve du zeles demonstrate, sometimes disobedience enhances efficiency or effectiveness: "Workers frequently violate standard rules and procedures in order to work more efficiently..." (Paul Goodman et al., op. cit., p. 117.) It is when such activity is taken by management as a slap in the face to their authority, as a statement that they are superfluous to the production process, that they react. And "reasonable" administrators will not react to disobedience which results in an increase in efficiency (except perhaps to change the policy to fit the "disobedient" behavior) unless the workers make plain their defiant attitude.

(152) Chester I. Barnard, op. cit., p. 169.

(153) William Ringle, "Teamsters Find Rebels Growing," Lafayette Journal and Courier (July 31, 1977), D-7.

5 Consequences and Policy

"Tut, tut, child," said the Duchess. "Everything's got a moral if only you can find it."

- Lewis Carroll, <u>Alice in Wonderland</u>

Bureaucratic oppositions are political phenomena that appear within social entities which are not supposed to be political systems. According to the administrative myth, the officials of a bureaucracy are primarily committed to the efficient and effective achievement of their public mission. They are responsible, through a board of directors, a board of trustees, or an elected official, to one or more broader constituencies. Their ultimate goals are provided for them by others, and their task is to make sure that these goals are fulfilled by developing specific policies and securing adequate implementation of them. If there are any obstacles to effective goal attainment, the administrators are supposed to be aware of them and to correct them. In terms of the administrative myth there should be no grounds for conflict within a bureaucracy, because employees are aware that they have no formal right to dispute the organization's public aims and administrators are motivated to achieve those aims efficiently and according to the rules. The ubiquity of bureaucratic oppositions shows that organizations are not self-corrective and, therefore, are not nonpolitical. They are, instead, seedbeds of conflict in which overt struggle is often muted by repression, just as it is in the authoritarian state, which also claims to have dispensed with politics.

The grounds for oppositions show that in contemporary organizations some employees do dispute the policies that specify general goals, though not usually the goals themselves, and that administrators often are not committed to the official aims of the organization, are not dedicated to efficient performance, and are not motivated to rectify even abuse that results from breach of the organization's own rules. For whatever motives an opposition may be initiated, it is usually possible to find abundant grounds for it and, perhaps, to induce such grounds. The conditions for political activity, then, are present within the everyday life of bureaucracies, though they may be concealed by widespread belief in the administrative myth and, more importantly, by fear of hierarchical power and habits of obedience that may originate in belief and fear. If the barriers to opposition are overcome, the administrative myth is dispelled, at least temporarily. Even the most innocent informer acknowledges, at least implicitly, that some abuses have escaped the attention of the authorities, that supervision is not all that it should be. In the ideal bureaucracy, "feedback" in the form of suggestions, praise, and reports of work output, not demands, is the only legitimate communication from the lower to the higher levels. Oppositions make demands, even if they are attenuated as tacit expectations that the authorities will act on information presented to them.

OPPOSITION AND AUTHORITY

Once a political process has been unleashed in a bureaucracy the first concerns of the authorities are to contain it within the organization, reassert the chain of command, and refurbish the administrative myth. They may also attempt to correct the abuses, but they will try to do so without admitting that there are abuses. Thus, they are not likely to reward oppositionists and tend to punish them even if they believe that the opposition was warranted. The authorities will attempt to depoliticize the situation as quickly as possible by suppressing conflict. They may do so through taking punitive measures, through making concessions, or through a combination of the two. Usually there will be some use of power and the main consequence of opposition will be reassertion of the hierarchy. Conditions, however, will not return to the status quo ante, because the political nature of the organization will have been revealed. All parties to the conflict will learn what a General Motors executive found out:

What is really involved is politics, the conscious sharing of control and power. History does not offer many examples of oligarchies that have abdicated with grace and good will. (1)

Of course, if the hierarchy fails to reassert itself effectively, the organization will have become politicized.

The "bureaucratic genius for retaliation" (2) is at its most creative in devising reprisals against those who mount oppositions. Among reprisals, personal attacks can be distinguished from job and career related measures. Aggression against persons includes various forms of physical attack and mental harassment, for which no authority is required. Vindictive administrators, who are anxious to maintain their control, often resemble schoolyard bullies or sadistic prison guards. Particularly, as in unions, where officials do not have authority over a dissident's working conditions, personal reprisals are likely to be used frequently.

For example, when several electrical workers tried and failed to rectify corruption in a local union, they "resigned from the union - determined not to

finance an organization whose leaders refused to account for its funds....
They were pelted with bolts and screws, punched, tripped, and burned with
cigarettes. Only a few friends of the three refused to take part in the
harassment." (3) The whistle blower, who attempts to go outside of the
organization to expose abuses, is particularly vulnerable to attack. Karen
Ann Silkwood may have been murdered to keep her from presenting
incriminating documents about the Kerr-McGee Corporation to the press.
(4)

Co-workers who interact with oppositionists are viewed as disloyal and are
subject to "guilt by association." Thus, there is a tendency to ostracize
dissenters. "The Amish know exactly what they are doing when they 'shun' a
brother; so do the Russians when they make a comrade a 'nonperson'." (5)
After blowing the whistle on the Air Force's cover-up of cost overruns Ernie
Fitzgerald returned to his office and found "the beginnings of a small pile of
call messages on his secretary's desk - each one a cancelled invitation to a
meeting, party, or dinner." (6)

Job and career related reprisals are more common measures against
oppositionists than physical and psychological attacks, because they allow
officials to use the organization's powers against isolated individuals or small
groups. Vindictive administrators need not commit themselves to a personal
conflict, but need only manipulate the rules and exercise their authority to
make the oppositionist's work life difficult or impossible. Attacks upon one's
career can be as damaging as physical or psychological assaults because work
provides the means to subsistence and leisure and, for many people, a purpose
for existence.

Dismissal is, of course, the most extreme job-related sanction and is a
measure frequently taken against dissidents. A psychiatric nurse who was
quoted in a news article as criticizing the quality of patient care and the
behavior of the medical staff at the Philadelphia hospital where she worked
was fired. (7) Also fired was a policeman who appeared on a television news
program and told about other police officers who had taken for their own use
recovered stolen property obtained in their regular course of duty. (8) A sales
executive at U.S. Steel blew the whistle on defective pipes and was
discharged. Ralph Nader and his associates analyzed this reprisal:

> The reason given: insubordination. Apparently, even though he may
> have saved the company substantial costs had the pipe been prema-
> turely marketed and saved users of the pipe from physical and
> financial injury, he had ignored the rules of the game and breached the
> etiquette of hierarchical management. (9)

Yet another example of retaliation by firing concerns a civilian doctor
working for the United States Army who blew the whistle. He charged that
there was "widespread negligence in military medical exams." The Army
expected him to handle 25 complete physicals each day, while he claimed that
only ten could be performed adequately. He was fired on the grounds of
inefficiency. (10)

In addition to being dismissed, oppositionists may also be denied letters of
recommendation or be blacklisted. In essence, they may be "exiled" from the
profession, craft, or career to which they have devoted much of their lives,
and, therefore, may suffer many of the same problems, frustrations, and

bitterness as political exiles.   Less severe measures of reprisal which also damage the individual materially and socially are demotions and, if there is a rating system, demerits.   Such formal reprisals are used when the authorities believe that they can act with impunity, free from the scrutiny of unions, civil service commissions, or other groups to which they might be answerable.

When it is not prudent for administrators to remove a dissident from a position, either by demotion or dismissal, their authority over the workplace can be used to make the conditions of employment difficult or intolerable for the targeted individual.   Such measures cannot be grounds for court cases or administrative actions because they are within the discretion of officials, and are usually not logged on the employee's permanent record.   Interference with a dissenter's work is a common bureaucratic practice, and is particularly prevalent in governmental agencies which are circumscribed by civil service regulations.   It can be used by immediate supervisors on their own initiative or as part of an overall plan involving top agency officials.   A congressional report referring specifically to whistle blowers employed by the federal government states: "Informal harassment can interfere with an employee's ability to do his work and result in disillusionment, resignation, or grounds for formal removal." (11)

The aim of interference with an individual's work can be to force the employee to resign, to set an example for other subordinates, or simply to get even with the dissenter.   The forms taken by such retaliation are myriad and can be especially painful to the recipients when they are tailor-made tortures, as were those described by George Orwell in 1984.   Many bureaucratic oppositionists initiate dissent just because they are dedicated to high standards of job performance.   Reprisals that prevent them from doing their work well are severe punishments.   For example, a high-level meat grader for the Food and Drug Administration made the "mistake" of helping to force the resignations of 70 percent of the Chicago meat graders by working with the FBI to prove their corruption.   Since his involvement he has been assigned a steady flow of assistant supervisors.   "By the time he finishes training one to be of any real assistance, transfer orders come in and the process starts again." (12)   J.A. Morris' bureaucratic opposition against the National Institutes of Health has been described previously.   He was opposed to the agency's policy of promoting flu vaccines because his own research led him to conclude that such programs were ineffective and potentially harmful. The hierarchy's reprisal was to prevent him from doing any research.   The authorities destroyed thousands of his experimental animals, forced him from his laboratory into a small room, and crated away his research materials. (13)

When the targeted employee is not a dedicated and committed worker there are other reprisals that can be taken by the administration.   Among employees in law enforcement agencies and school systems the measure most feared is transfer to an undesirable area where, for example, the likelihood of physical attack is high.   The power of corporations to make punitive transfers is discussed by Anthony Jay.   Employees "can be told to go and live in another part of the country, or another part of the world, or to desert their wives and children for months or years ...." (14)   The authorities also have discretion over perquisites, which are not only valued for their intrinsic worth, but for the status-honor that they confer.   Corner offices, a private secretary instead of the typing pool, a convenient parking space, travel, and flexible schedules are some of the privileges of certain jobs that give satisfaction and that may be revoked.

More general measures of reprisal involve the denial of possibilities for promotion and salary increases. Advancement on the organizational ladder is largely a function of loyalty. Critical analysts of bureaucracy claim that "individual workers gain promotion only by manifesting managerially-defined norms of behavior and commitment and by accepting, without protest or grumbling, authoritative commands from above." (15) The individual's performance is often difficult to evaluate, so promotion is frequently granted on the basis of loyalty to superiors and social conformity. Robert Presthus concurs:

> For various reasons, including the desire to preserve internal unity and discipline, LOYALTY seems to have become the main basis for bureaucratic succession. (16)

Presthus interprets bureaucracies "as miniature social systems that meet many of the most basic needs of their members and expect in return loyalty and conformity." (17) Thus, punishing bureaucratic oppositionists by failing to promote them, despite their competence, is a "natural" reprisal.

The retaliatory measures against oppositionists may be more or less severe. Assuming that the authorities are instrumentally rational, one would expect in return the strength of reprisals to be commensurate with or at least relative to the real or potential damage done by the opposition to the administration. Bureaucratic oppositions which are grounded in policy abuses rather than in rule violations, which have goals of policy change rather than of personnel change, and which utilize tactics that reveal the opposition to outside agencies rather than keep it within the organization are more dangerous to the hierarchy of authority and tend to call forth more severe retaliation. Similarly, open political tactics threaten the chain of command more than informing and, thus, will tend to be more severely suppressed.

Organizational reprisals against bureaucratic oppositionists may serve purposes other than retribution and deterrence. Administrative measures may be counter attacks to repulse the opposition's assault, to prevent the erosion of authority, and to stave off the changes in policy or personnel that are the aims of the opposition. When the authorities attempt to damage the reputations of dissenters they not only harm the individuals but diminish their political effectiveness. Such techniques of character assassination are spelled out in a manuscript known as the "Malek Manual," which was written for Nixon appointees with the intention of helping them rule the federal agencies. The measures advised in the Malek Manual are "designed to focus attention on the employee and not his or her allegations." (18) The strategy is similar to that used against rebels in the polity. "The rebel is depicted in negative terms by society, labeled 'irrational,' 'degenerate,' or at least 'irresponsible.'" (19)

Destroying the reputations of dissidents robs them of credibility, while transferring them may deprive them of access to the evidence needed to prove the existence of an abuse. The Malek Manual laments the difficulty of firing federal bureaucrats - "Political disloyalty and insimpatico relationships with the Administration, unfortunately, are not grounds for the removal or suspension of an employee." (20) Therefore, a number of suggestions are made for neutralizing the employee, such as the "special assignment technique (the traveling salesman)," "the layering technique," and the "shifting responsibilities and isolation techniques." The Manual condones covert threats to fire, transfer, or demote employees, which may cause oppositionists to abandon their project. (21)

Retaliation by the administration is the organizational counterpart of punitive sanctions in society at large. Reprisals are social control mechanisms used to keep people in line when more pervasive inducements and penalties, such as monetary reward, career advancement, social approval, and guilt fail to elicit obedience. They are political tactics just as are the maneuvers of the dissidents. A comparison of opposition tactics with administrative reprisals shows just how many more resources are at the disposal of the authorities than are available to their subordinates.

Successful retaliation by the administration against a bureaucratic opposition reasserts the organization's chain of command and is a signal to dissenters that future activities will be costly and likely to fail. In many cases, then, the consequences of opposition include a lower probability that open conflict will break out again. There are many reasons why opposition may not be self perpetuating. Most important, unless the authorities are irrational in their use of power, they will have learned how to prevent new troubles by being alert to their causes. Perhaps they will rectify the abuse, but they may also learn how to cover it up better or devise new work rules that monitor employees more closely, deprive them of access to information, or punish dissent more severely. In some cases the budget of a rebellious department may be cut or certain of its perquisites revoked, putting the members on notice that they are not indispensable and that they no longer have high status-honor. The ringleaders of the opposition may be fired, hounded out of the organization, or transferred, removing the potential initiators of future dissent and destroying the solidarity of the struggle group. Exemplary punishments may be meted out, showing employees what they can expect if they disobey, or certain oppositionists may be coopted, weakening the morale of the remaining members.

Cooptation is a popular tactic for suppressing future conflict because it allows the organization to keep an individual with leadership skills and also destroys the mutual trust among dissenters necessary to maintain an opposition.

There are many ways to coopt incumbents who emerge with views inconsistent with existing ones.... conflict may be resolved by establishing a small program of the type proposed.... Over time, the proposal backers may find that the ideas are less workable than they originally thought and the unit may simply be disbanded. Thus, cooptation is less dramatic than...overt dismissal, but may well have the same effect of resolving the strain without preciptating any type of structural change. (22)

In addition to any measures directly taken by the authorities, the very process of opposition often has a chilling effect on future political activity. The costs of opposition in time, peace of mind, congeniality, ability to do effective work, and, perhaps, even money and health only become apparent after the struggle has been initiated. Having suffered such costs, former oppositionists may be reluctant ever to challenge organizational authority again. The will to resist may be replaced by bitterness (especially if one's friends have been fired or punished), cynicism, apathy, or expediency ("If you can't beat 'em, join 'em!"). New employees who might initiate action will enter a demoralized social context, and will be unable to inspire the zeal to resist authority.

The very social relations among oppositionists may further dampen the will to resist future abuses or to continue resisting abuses that have not been corrected. Particularly in protracted oppositions, the members of the group will differentiate themselves by their willingness to take risks, to support their comrades emotionally, and to spend time devising tactics and politicking. Jealousies and rivalries may build up based on differential contributions to the common effort. Some members may give in to the authorities and be branded as traitors, while others may escalate the conflict and be branded as hotheads. People will also reveal the weaknesses in their characters under stress and may be humiliated in front of their colleagues. By the time some protracted oppositions are over, their members will have such animosity and distrust towards one another that future collaboration will be ruled out. Opposition may sometimes be inspiring but it is rarely pleasant. Even when struggle is successful group solidarity may be destroyed:

> A group's complete victory over its enemies is thus not always fortunate in the sociological sense. Victory lowers the energy which guarantees the unity of the group; and the dissolving forces, which are always at work, gain hold. (23)

When the authorities are able to suppress an opposition thoroughly, the chain of command will be vindicated but the performance of the organization may suffer. Successful reprisals demonstrate the brute power of the administration to overcome dissent, but they do not enhance feelings of obligation and loyalty to the organization. An opposition may fail and may even make future struggles less likely to occur, but organizational functioning may become less efficient. Obedience to organizational rules on the basis of fear rather than on the grounds of legitimacy has several interrelated results. First, employees will respect only the letter, not the spirit, of the rules. The consequence is similar to a greve du zele action. In most bureaucracies the rules must be supplemented by common sense and used as flexible guidelines rather than cookbook-style instructions. Over-rigid adherence to them generally impairs efficiency. The informal practices which normally emerge to shore up or complement official orders are either purposefully neglected out of fear of reprisals or spite, or are not even considered. Development of informal procedures requires both creativity and extra energy, both of which are inhibited by fear. Presthus reflects on the effects of the anxiety to please superiors that is caused by fear:

Since the elite is remote and its will cannot always be definitely known, the individual attempts to anticipate its expectations. As a result such expectations may seem more compelling than they are meant to be. The individual is not inclined in any case to underestimate them for fear of impairing his career chances. In this way organizational claims may be expanded beyond reason. Here the federal government's loyalty-security program is illustrative. The going rationale was, "Don't take a chance, kick 'em in the pants." This rule of exaggerated response is a major dysfunction of big organizations. (24)

Similarly, fearful or apathetic employees are unlikely to report inefficiencies to higher authorities, thus depriving administrators of valuable "feedback."

A second consequence of obedience from fear is a tendency for employees to break rules when they believe that they will not be caught ("When the cat's away the mice will play."). In a study of boys working under varying conditions of authority, noncompliance increased greatly when the autocratic leader left the room. (25) The implication of this research is that obedience requires constant supervision when it is obtained through fear. When an organization gains obedience by implicit or explicit threat, it becomes similar to a police state which must continually monitor its citizens and expend appreciable resources to do so. The more closely an organization must supervise its personnel, the less efficient it will be. Employees will take less productive initiative and managerial overhead will increase. Authoritarian states may have as their primary aim the assertion of a chain of command. Organizational elites must usually seek other goals in addition to maintaining control.

A final consequence of obedience obtained through fear, particularly obedience to rules or superiors perceived to be abusive, is impairment of the mental and/or physical health of the employee.

They'd like to tell off their bosses but don't know how to do it. They evade and repress their great dislike of the situation because they feel powerless to win out over the boss. This often leads to illness, frequent absenteeism, regular tardiness, and poor work habits. (26)

Obviously such reactions damage both the efficiency and the effectiveness of the organization.

The creation of a climate of fear in the wake of an opposition demonstrates the power of the organization's hierarchy but weakens, at least temporarily, its legitimate authority. It is difficult to generalize about the long-term effects of the exercise of brute power in organizations. If the opposition is isolated and its ring leaders are dismissed or otherwise neutralized harsh reprisals will probably strengthen the authority system over the long range, because employees will be aware that officials are prepared to assert themselves decisively when they are challenged. If, however, oppositions are frequent or the organization as a whole is corrupt, inefficient, or otherwise abusive, stringent retaliation against a particular group of dissidents will feed a cycle of demoralization and inefficiency. Whether such a cycle is damaging to the authorities depends upon their commitment to the official goals of the organization and the pressure of constituencies and governmental agencies on them to achieve those goals.

Oppositions, of course, are not always effectively suppressed by organizational authorities. Sometimes they are successful in eliminating the abuses that they have fought and sometimes they win concessions from higher authorities. When dissidents are successful, believe that they have succeeded, or are not dispirited by administrative reprisals, they may create a political culture at the workplace, making future oppositions more likely. While suppressed dissent generally leads to demoralization, at least in the short run, opposition that is not crushed generates the belief among employees that they need not obey authorities without question, that they have some power over their conditions or even over the policies that they execute. A successful opposition within one department of an organization may serve as a model for others to emulate, thereby weakening the chain of command. If it has been well enough publicized, an opposition may even be imitated in other organizations.

Whether or not a bureaucratic opposition has achieved its goal, it may help to make future oppositions possible by providing a base of employees who can be mobilized for action. One of the major difficulties in undertaking an opposition is finding employees who are willing to act and then forming them into a cohesive group. To the extent that the previous opposition group remains solidary and politically motivated, the likelihood of future oppositions is enhanced. During the first struggle the tactics used may have led to a strong camaraderie and trust among the group members that remained after the group's combat function was discarded. For example, tactics that involve secrecy among the members, such as anonymous informing or making a superior appear to be incompetent, often provide a sense of solidarity. This result has been noted by those studying secret societies. (27)

Past exploits may lead to the continued coherence of the group, not merely because the members share a common experience, but because of the negative reaction of their colleagues. It is understandable that a state of mutual animosity usually exists between those involved in the opposition and those who might have been but refused to take part. Such hostile feelings may linger long after the conclusion of the opposition and may serve to perpetuate the group, if only because of the enmity they receive from and feel towards the "scabs." In such cases the dissolution of the group from its internal tensions will be avoided.

From a sociological viewpoint, the broadest generalization that can be drawn about the consequences of bureaucratic oppositions is that they tend to weaken the legitimate authority of the organization over at least some of its employees. Max Weber, who was primarily concerned with the authority of the state, argued that the grounds of legitimacy could be traditional (from inherited custom), charismatic (from the personal gift of a leader), or legal-rational (from a set of procedures). Although bureaucracies develop traditions and sometimes are taken over by charismatic figures, their major basis of authority in the Weberian scheme is legal-rational. Thus, their legitimacy can be impaired if their officials break the rules or if subordinates challenge the rules.

The fundamental proposition that rule infractions weaken bureaucratic authority must be modified to account for the consequences of bureaucratic oppositions. First, bureaucracies do not depend for their legitimacy only upon legal-rational authority. Their rules must not merely be formally consistent and explicit, but they must also promote the organization's pursuit of its official aims. Thus, bureaucratic authority is both legal-rational and instrumental-rational. There may be a conflict between these two grounds for legitimacy when there is question about whether the formal rules serve the organization's purposes. Some bureaucratic oppositions challenge legal-rational authority in order to promote instrumental-rational authority, others are aimed against officials who violate the rules, and still others are aimed at officials who do not apply the rules effectively.

For the administrative myth, the rules of the organization are instrumentally adapted to its goals and the officials apply those rules universally and effectively. The conditions for myth to approximate reality include the requirement that the goals be clear and consistent. If multiple and contradictory aims can be imputed to the organization, its legitimacy may be impaired by dissensus over which should be given priority. For example, the engineers who exposed the dangers of nuclear reactors believed that General Electric should not profit at the expense of public safety. (28) Similarly, the whistle blower who informed the District Attorney in Brooklyn that the Good Humor Corporation was marketing ice cream with high bacteria counts believed that a safe product was more important than high profits. (29) In both these cases, the authority of the organization was challenged on the grounds of value rationality, not on the grounds of instrumental rationality. (30) Thus, a second modification of Weber's scheme must include the possibility that an organization's legitimacy is rooted in the purposes that it pursues as well as in its formal consistency and its efficiency and effectiveness. Some employees may be committed to the goals that the organization actually achieves, others may mount oppositions when the actual goals conflict with the official purposes, and still others may dissent against practices that breach moral standards. In the last case it is claimed that a moral ideal should be the supreme goal of the organization or that it should at least limit the pursuit of its other aims.

Rule infractions, then, only necessarily weaken the organization's authority when a) there is agreement on the organization's goals, b) the rules are instrumentally rational with regard to those goals, and c) officials pursue those goals competently and effectively. If any of these three conditions are not met, rule infractions may or may not weaken the organization's legitimate authority, depending upon the specific circumstances. For example, the overall authority of an organization may be strengthened when employees are permitted to bend or break the rules in order to achieve greater efficiency, or when the organization departs from its official goal in order to provide more jobs at the sacrifice of efficiency.

Bureaucratic oppositions, then, do not weaken legitimate organizational authority merely because they may break some of the rules, but because they challenge the chain of command. Whatever effects oppositions may have that strengthen overall authority in the long run, they always impair the principle of hierarchy in the short run. They show that the authorities have not been wise enough to assure obedience, and, thus, they expose the weakness of the structure. Even if an opposition is crushed, it turns the organization into more of a power system than it was previously. In essence, bureaucratic opposition creates a gap between the maintenance of order and the purposes of work, between power and goodness, between "project orientation" and "object orientation." (31) It politicizes the organization by opening up disputes over goals, the means to achieve goals, or the effective use of means. For as long as the opposition lasts subordinates take a responsibility for the organization that is not theirs by formal right.

Opposition, then, reveals that some authorities have not been responsible, that they have allowed grounded abuses to exist and that they have created conditions in which subordinates can act to try to rectify those abuses. A functionalist might argue against the interpretation that successful oppositions could increase the legitimacy of the chain of command by eliminating incompetent or abusive personnel, by achieving the alteration of inefficient practices, or by recommitting the organization to its official goals. All of these effects may occur and may help to strengthen legitimacy in the long run, but they will not eliminate the short-run effect of politicizing the organization. The functionalist might reply that the public punishment of rule violators, the reasonable alteration of rules, or the rededication to official aims may convince subordinates of the essential goodness of the authorities and reinforce normative solidarity. It is difficult to assess the strength of this argument, but it may be noted that public rectification of abuses promotes solidarity most in communities whose members share an identity of interest and have a "consciousness of kind." In such communities public punishment makes the norms conspicuous by singling out isolated deviants from the rest of the community, by focusing attention upon the "exceptions who prove the rule." Organizations are hierarchies, not communities. Admission by officials that oppositionists were right probably casts doubt upon their competence more than it creates solidarity. Such admission may also reveal that the abuses are not exceptions, but the rule.

If oppositions are made public, they also impair the legitimate authority of the organization in the wider society which may lead to new legal controls over it, loss of its effectiveness with clients or customers, or decline in its status. Statements by officials that abuses have been or will be corrected cannot, in the short run, counterbalance the suspicions created among those who are affected by or are dependent on the organization. Further, oppositions alert those outside the organization that the chain of command has been challenged and that the authorities may not be able to speak for the agency competently or carry out their promises. This consequence of opposition is probably the basic reason why officials are so concerned that dissent be suppressed before it escalates and broadens its range beyond the organization. In a competitive environment the organization must speak with one voice lest its adversaries sense weakness and take advantage of it.

The belief that opposition might hurt the organization's public standing has even prevented the initiation of some bureaucratic oppositions, because the effectiveness of the organization has consequences for the welfare of the subordinates. Stanley Weir, in an analysis of the International Longshoreman's Workers Union, concluded that this belief is responsible for

... the refusal of the working longshoremen to air the problems of their union in public. They have felt that the ensuing scandal would create a reactionary offensive against the job-hiring process which the ILWU controls jointly with the stevedoring companies.... (32)

The vital tension of bureaucratic opposition springs from the fact that in all organizations there are wide deviations from the administrative ideal, and yet that attempts to correct these deviations from below weaken the chain of command and invite disorder. The same sort of tension marks all authoritarian systems, because they do not institutionalize opposition. Such systems rely on control from above and when that control fails the system itself must be disrupted to correct abuses. When abuses become systemic, the entire system must be revised or an unjust and stagnant order maintained. In democratic systems there are ways of airing grievances, publicizing abuses, and altering policies in an orderly fashion, so opposition in them need not always threaten legitimate authority. Organizations, which are predominantly authoritarian systems, are structurally incapable of taking full advantage of the benefits of opposition. Their first concern is to suppress.

POLICY

Bureaucratic oppositions, particularly those that have occurred in public agencies, have alerted legislators, constituencies, and the general public to organizational abuses. The melioristic impulse is strong in the United States; many people believe that the recognition of a problem, an evil, or a lack requires self-conscious intervention to set things right. In the view of the reformer it should be possible to provide an orderly means of eliminating, preventing, or at least lessening the abuses that have been exposed by the irregular tactics of oppositions. The preceding discussion has argued that whether or not oppositions are successful, their general effect is to weaken the organization's chain of command. Proposals to provide new agencies to perform the functions of oppositions or to make certain oppositions legitimate will have the same effect of weakening the administrative hierarchy. The most basic question of policy directed at remediating organizational abuses, then, is whether or not it is desirable, or even feasible, to diminish the autonomy of contemporary hierarchies. Some insight into the dimensions of this question will result from considering how administrative autonomy is currently limited.

In addition to the threat of bureaucratic oppositions, administrators in complex societies are constrained by a wide variety of factors to eliminate sadistic, insecure, or incompetent personnel, to promote efficiency and effectiveness, and to refrain from making and implementing illegal, though not always immoral, policy. First, bureaucracies are enmeshed in a competitive environment. Businesses must normally return a reasonable rate of profit to continue operating, and if they are "bailed out" of trouble by government they are likely to suffer increased regulation. Colleges and hospitals must have adequate enrollments and reasonable rates of occupancy or they face diminished contributions or budget cuts. Even governmental agencies, which are monopolies, must compete against one another for shares of budgets, and must at least appear to achieve a certain standard of performance. Competitive controls are minimized for businesses which are monopoly suppliers of an important product or service and for governmental agencies concerned with security, such as the CIA. In both cases, a veil of secrecy inhibits effective oversight.

A second limitation on administrative autonomy is public regulation through legislative oversight, independent regulatory agencies, executive control, or the court system. Ever since the Progressive era at the beginning of the twentieth century, many measures have been taken to correct organizational abuses by employing the countervailing power of the public sector. The preceding discussion has shown that government controls have not prevented abuses that generate bureaucratic oppositions, though it has not demonstrated that such controls have failed to lessen the number of abuses or their severity. Often organizations have "colonized" regulatory authorities with sympathetic personnel or have "captured" them in order to use them as tools for their own advantage. Even in such cases, however, competing interests have gained some leverage over the administrative hierarchy, reducing its autonomy.

A third set of restrictions on bureaucratic autonomy is provided by organized interest groups and lateral organizations, such as civil rights groups, consumer movements, unions, and professional associations. Whether or not limitations on administrative power are written into contracts, as they sometimes are when an organization is checked by a union, or into consent decrees, as they are when interest groups bring successful suits, hierarchies are circumscribed by lateral organizations merely by the threats of decreased support or of attempts to seek legislative remedies. The preceding chapters have shown that lateral organizations have been no more successful than government agencies in preventing abuses but, again, it has not argued that such interest groups have been entirely ineffective.

The present study of bureaucratic oppositions has been biased in the direction of demonstrating just how ineffective the checks on complex organizations have been. However, the conclusion need not be drawn that more of the same kinds of checks would rectify more of the abuses, or that there are other kinds of constraints, consistent with the present order, that have not yet been tried. Current measures have perhaps not been successful, because the condition for effectiveness would be the destruction of the organization as an authoritarian system. Those who offer policy proposals to correct organizational abuses will find that their plans fall into one of two categories: either they will merely repeat previous efforts or they will alter the current authority system so much as to change the hierarchical principle radically. If the first is the case, then the organization will still have the autonomy to perpetrate and conceal abuses, barring opposition, while if the second is the intent the present system itself will be put in question.

A few oppositionists and commentators have been aware of the dilemma of reform and have advocated drastic measures. In certain cases there have been proposals to eliminate the offending organization altogether. For example, the nuclear engineers who resigned from General Electric because they realized that nuclear safety was not technologically feasible joined forces with anti-nuclear groups to urge legislation to ban all atomic plants. (33) Similarly, a group whose goal is the destruction of the CIA includes some former CIA employees, including Philip Agee.   Its plans involve the establishment of "a worldwide network of agents to expose CIA personnel and methods of operation." (34)   Such attempts to abolish organizations, of course, only apply to special cases and cannot be applied universally, unless alternative ways of performing collective tasks are proposed and implemented.

Sometimes oppositionists can create a new organization that is intended either to supplant the old one or to compete with it successfully enough to spur changes.   Such schismatic initiatives are beyond the capabilities of most employees, either because of the enormous capital investment required to start a new organization or because of the guaranteed monopoly of government agencies.   There are some organizations where the possibility exists, particularly those which are skill rather than capital intensive, such as consulting firms, advertising agencies, and especially religious organizations.

Papal authority was critically diminished by Martin Luther's bureaucratic opposition.   Protestant asceticism makes schisms practicable because an ornate church is not required.   The abundance of sects now in existence is witness to the feasibility of starting new religious organizations. A group of "moderates who believed they had become the victims of an 'ecclesiastical tyranny'" within the Lutheran Church-Missouri Synod split from the Church's Concordia Theological Seminary in St. Louis. (35)   A "seminary in exile" was established and thousands of church members were reformed into new congregations.   The leadership of the parent Church then declared the opposition group to be a separate church. (36)

Radical and comprehensive change has been suggested by those who propose substituting participatory democracy at the workplace for the principle of hierarchy.   The program of worker self-management involves

... the full and direct participation of every working member in decisions which vitally affect him.   ... It involves the full decision-making process of discussion and selection of alternatives, coming to agreement, implementing, and assessing consequences. (37)

Substituting participation for hierarchical authority attacks the very heart of the bureaucracy.   Higher administrators would no longer enjoy the secrecy necessary to perpetrate many abuses.   As Weber noted, "Bureaucratic administration always tends to be an administration of 'secret sessions': insofar as it can, it hides its knowledge and action from criticism." (38) Democracy in the organization means the institutionalization of opposition. It is the only plan that would dissolve the dilemma of authoritarian politics, because it would eliminate them.

It is beyond the scope of the present study to assess the practicability or the desirability of worker self-management.   The theoretical and empirical literature about the subject is large and growing. (39) It is important to note here, however, that democratic machinery does not itself insure actual democracy, as unions and many local governments illustrate.   Employee "culture," the imperatives of technology, and the political and economic climate in which an organization is embedded are just some of the factors that need to be considered in any discussion about the possibility of democratizing orgnaizations. Further, in order to give worker self-management a "fair chance" it would have to be universalized, which would demand both a socialist economy and new forms of citizen-controlled public institutions. Such a radical change may be desirable, but it is not currently a "live option," at least in the United States.

Most suggestions for eliminating organizational abuses are efforts to work within the present system of controls and constraints. The most popular proposals concentrate on rectifying the specific abuses that have been exposed by extending the kinds of regulatory mechanisms developed since the Progressive era to cover them. For example, instituting a Cabinet Department of Consumer Affairs or strengthening the Consumer Product Safety Commission is a proposed response to revelations about hazardous products. Similarly, there have been calls to reform the Civil Service Commission to enable administrators to more easily dismiss incompetent employees. Such measures have been repeatedly tested for more than 50 years in a wide variety of contexts. As noted above, their success has been limited by the autonomy of the organization's administration. Target organizations will attempt to colonize or capture regulatory authorities and to blunt their effectiveness. If their efforts are unsuccessful some abuses may be corrected, but perhaps at the cost of efficiency or effectiveness.

Similar to government regulation and tightened public controls are measures that increase the power of lateral organizations over the target bureaucracy. For example, various women's groups, such as the National Organization for Women, Working Women United, and the Women's Equity Action League, provide how-to information and legal aid to oppositions fighting superiors who sexually harass their female subordinates, or policies which discriminate against female employees. Ralph Nader and his associates call for the encouragement of bureaucratic oppositionists by professional societies and instruct these groups to "reformulate their codes of ethics to make them relevant to the employment relationship as well as to the client-professional relationship." (40) Professional associations and unions may also provide legal aid for members employed in abusive organizations. A self-help organization has been formed "to provide assistance to all employees of security-related agencies who wish to come forth and expose inefficiency or illegality in the outfit they work for. Legal assistance for the new organization will be provided by the American Civil Liberties Union...." (41)

The American Chemical Society has proposed the institution of a legal aid fund to help oppositionists resist abusive practices. The Society's president argued:

We are aware of many cases in industry, government laboratories and even universities where scientists have been retaliated against when their professional standards interfered with the interests of their employers or funders. (42)

Chemists who opposed their organization's policies in the name of their professional standards would be able to fight retaliation from their superiors in the courts with the ACS's aid.

Some bureaucratic oppositions have led to the formation of lateral groups to check the offending organization. One such example is the Teamster reform group mentioned earlier, PROD. In the main, PROD regularizes the informing tactics of many bureaucratic oppositions. One of its efforts was to support Teamster members in a New Jersey local who were being coerced into contributing money to the legal defense committee for Anthony Provenzano. (43) He had once headed the local, but had been convicted in court of murder and extortion. His victim had been his major rival for leadership in the union. Members of the local were far too intimidated to oppose the policy themselves but PROD was able to act on their behalf. Its tactic was to inform to the Justice Department. A letter was sent to the organized crime and racketeering section head by Paul Poulos, PROD's organizing director - " ... Poulos said his group has received calls and letters from union members who believe they will face hardships on the job if they do not contribute to Provenzano's defense." (44)

While the example of PROD shows some of the limitations of unionism, the result of a few bureaucratic oppositions is the formation of a union to provide a regular check on perceived abuses. If a union does emerge from a bureaucratic opposition it is likely that the struggle was unsuccessful. Had the dissidents achieved their goal they would not have seen the need to continue to commit resources to a conflict. Some outsiders, unaware of the failed attempt to oust President Silber, could not understand why Boston University's faculty chose to unionize. An insider grasped the situation:

> "This is the most status-anxious faculty," says one of the Silber's deans. "They are more royal than the king, more papal than the pope. For this faculty to have embraced unionism prior to John Silber was unthinkable." (45)

Just as government regulation has a long history, so does the use of pressure by lateral organizations. The consequence of such pressure may be to lessen certain abuses, but unless the lateral organization shares power with the target bureaucracy it will probably not eliminate them. If the target bureaucracy is able to coopt the lateral organization it will probably be even more difficult than before for subordinates to resist abuses. The same conclusion applies to regulatory agencies that are colonized or captured by the regulated. If the target bureaucracy is not successful at cooptation then it may lost efficiency because of the measures it takes to satisfy organized interests. The values promoted and sacrificed by both government regulation and intervention by lateral organization will depend on the balance of power in each concrete situation. In general, reformers might remember Santayana's dictum:

> A thousand reforms have left the world as corrupt as ever, for each successful reform has founded a new institution, and this institution has bred its new and congenial abuses. (46)

The use of government regulation and lateral groups to check organizational abuses relies upon bringing external power to bear upon the target bureaucracy, forestalling the need for spontaneous opposition from within or at least giving such opposition leverage outside of the organization. Another sort of proposal for change is aimed at modifying the internal structure of the organization to provide new channels for reporting abuses or legal protection for those who blow the whistle. A law professor has, for example, suggested the creation of

> full-time, well-staffed in-house probation officers which are either appointed by the courts or regulatory agencies, and who are designated to receive bad news. (47)

Such an official, similar to the ombundsman, would be a projection of outside agencies into the organization. Depending on the powers assigned to the office, the organization's hierarchy would be more or less impaired. At one extreme there would merely be a new conduit for information and at the other there would be authority over management, such as is exerted in the Soviet Union by Communist Party "control commissions." The same dilemma applies to this proposal as to the other, more traditional, measures. If the organization coopts the new office, then oppositionists will be more reluctant to initiate action, but if the office is not coopted, the administration will lose authority, not necessarily to subordinates, but to an external agency which may itself be abusive. In the case of "public directors," there would be multiple centers of authority within the organization, breaking the chain of command.

Perhaps the most popular new remedy for organizational abuses is the provision of legal protection from reprisals for employees who wish to blow the whistle. Basic to this reform is the extension to employees of some constitutional rights that now exist only for citizens. Law professor David Ewing, in his book Freedom Inside the Organization: Bringing Civil Liberties to the Workplace, calls for the following in a "bill of rights for organization people" - "freedom to criticize a company's social and ethical policies. Freedom to object to an immoral or unethical directive." (48) Ewing argues that

> The First Amendment need not and should not be applied to all forms of employee speech and writing. If it is applied just to questions of social responsibility, morality, and ethics, the need is met. Then those who know first and most about questionable corporate plans and practices would be free to challenge management without losing their jobs and chances for promotion. (49)

Bills submitted to the Ninety-fifth Congress attempted to provide such rights to employees of the federal government. For example, the coordinated Senate bill, S. 3108, sponsored by Senators Leahy, Humphrey, and Abourezk would " ... provide for the protection of government employees who disclose information of illegal or improper actions within the government" by setting up a Merit Systems Protection Board to investigate complaints about abuses and to restore "aggrieved" employees to their status prior to improper disciplinary action. For private employees, a writer in a management journal suggests that the corporation "should develop around a 'constitution' that establishes the rights of the individual and the limitation of the power of the organization over him." (50)

Except for the suggestion that organizations be made constitutional, which would acknowledge them to be political systems and change their present form, the proposals to grant and protect employee rights are not substantially different from the creation of "public directors." Such rights, to be effective, would have to be enforced by an agency, perhaps a "merit systems protection board," which would be able to enter the organization, investigate it, and discipline it in certain areas of administration. Short of some form of self-management, subordinates who mount oppositions must rely on their own wits or on the power of some external agency. A new external agency to hear and perhaps redress complaints about abuses would probably suffer the same fate as the Inspector General in the Armed Services. The ineffectiveness of the Inspector General, discussed previously, was attributed primarily to the impossibility of maintaining a dual structure of authority in a hierarchical organization. Just as in the case of the "public director," a merit systems protection board would inhibit opposition if it were weak or coopted, or would take control of the organization if it followed the Soviet model of control commissions. Under present conditions in the United States the former alternative would be the more likely outcome.

All of the proposed reforms of bureaucratic abuses which work within the present system confront a basic dilemma. The ground of hierarchical administrative authority is that a specific group of officials should be held responsible for the conduct and performance of the organization. The chain of command is a way of localizing and fixing responsibility. The presence of abuses within organizations shows that in many cases the officials cannot or will not behave responsibly, or that their interpretation of responsible behavior differs from that of other groups or individuals. Reform of abuses concentrates on making officials accountable to other agencies. Such accountability, however, weakens their autonomy or, in the case of cooption, allows them to be even more abusive and less accountable than they were before. Reform, then, diffuses responsibility and gives officials excuses for their failures. They may actually become so hedged by regulations and pressures that they cannot act effectively, or they may be able to blame other agencies for their own misdeeds. Meanwhile there is no guarantee that subordinates and publics will suffer any less abuse. Yet the call for reform responds to a situation in which the competitive controls which supposedly undergird organizational society have failed. It is, indeed, a vicious circle.

The choice seems to be between abusive organizations which maintain their chains of command, and irresponsible organizations in which authority is fragmented and diffused among plural agencies and groups - either "decentralized totalitarianism" or "hyper-pluralism." Much of the reason for this prospect lies in the deep social conflicts in contemporary societies over the purposes that organizations should serve. Within this atmosphere of division no consistent "public" policy for rectifying abuses can be formulated. Each measure will help some groups and hinder others. Those who disapprove of the aims of current organizational elites will welcome the fragmentation of their power, while those who approve of those aims will deplore it. Probably nothing will stop the abuses, or the spontaneous oppositions against them.

In the light of the policy alternatives, bureaucratic oppositions take on a more favorable appearance. They respond to specific situations flexibly, show people that at least for a moment they can resist, sometimes create systems of shared power, and keep elites aware that their employees are persons, not "cheerful robots." Bureaucratic oppositions fulfill more closely than any other contemporary social phenomena the Jeffersonian ideal of human beings freely and periodically asserting their liberty against tyrannical structures.   To attempt to regularize them would deprive them of their essence and deliver them to dependence upon other hierarchies. To "manage" them into submission would be to take another long step towards the one-dimensional society, the "crystal palace." To give them friendly encouragement, with a dash of realism, has been the purpose of this book.

CHAPTER 5: NOTES

(1) Emma Rothschild, Paradise Lost: The Decline of the Auto-Industrial Age, New York: Random House, 1973, p. 163.

(2) William Proxmire as quoted in Ralph Nader, Peter J. Petkas and Kate Blackwell, Whistle Blowing: The Report of the Conference on Professional Responsibility. New York: Grossman Publishers, 1972, p. 14.

(3) Kenneth Y. Tomlinson, "The Lonely Ordeal of Dale Richardson," Reader's Digest 106 (May 1975): 125-26.

(4) B.J. Phillips, "The Case of Karen Silkwood: The Mysterious Death of a Nuclear Plant Worker," Ms 3, #10 (April 1975): 59-66.

(5) Richard Reeves, "The Last Angry Man," Esquire (March 1, 1978): 42.

(6) Ibid.

(7) Kenneth D. Walters, "Your Employees' Right to Blow the Whistle," Harvard Business Review 53, #4 (July-August 1975): 28.

(8) Ibid.

(9) Ralph Nader et al., op. cit., p. 155.

(10) "Doctor Charges Army Exams Lax," Lafayette Journal and Courier (July 31, 1978): 1.

(11) United States Senate Committee on Governmental Affairs, The Whistle-Blowers: A Report on Federal Employees Who Disclose Acts of Government Waste, Abuse and Corruption, Washington, D.C.: U.S. Government Printing Office, February 1978, p. 27.

(12) Ibid., p. 29.

(13) Alexander Cockburn and James Ridgeway, "Scientist J. Anthony Morris-He Fought the Flu Shots and the U.S. Fired Him," Long Island Press (Parade Magazine) (March 13, 1977): 20.

(14) Antony Jay, Management and Machiavelli: An Inquiry into the Politics of Corporate Life, New York: Bantam Books, 1968, p. 16.

(15) Paul Goodman and Donald R. Van Houten, "Managerial Strategies and the Worker: A Marxist Analysis of Bureaucracy," Sociological Quarterly 18 (Winter 1977): 116.

(16) Robert Presthus, The Organizational Society: An Analysis and a Theory, New York: Vintage-Random, 1962, p. 49.

(17) Ibid., p. 95.

(18) United States Senate Committee on Governmental Affairs, op. cit., pp. 26-27.

(19) James V. Downton Jr., Rebel Leadership: Commitment and Charisma in the Revolutionary Process. New York: Free Press, 1973, p. 70.

(20) Quoted in United States Senate Committee on Governmental Affairs, op. cit., p. 382.

(21) Ibid., p. 27.

(22) J. Eugene Hass and Thomas E. Drabek, Complex Organizations: A Sociological Perspective, New York: Macmillan, 1973, p. 289.

(23) Georg Simmel, Conflict and the Web of Group-Affiliations. Glencoe: Free Press, 1955, p. 98.

(24) Robert Presthus, op. cit., pp. 146-47.

(25) Ralph White and Ronald Lippitt, "Leader Behavior and Member Reaction in Three 'Social Climates,'" Group Dynamics: Research and Theory, Dorwin Cartwright and Alvin Zander (eds.), Evanston: Row Peterson, 1953, pp. 585-611.

(26) Jack Houston, "Learning How to Get Along with the Boss," Chicago Tribune (August 10, 1975): section 12, p. 1.

(27) For an excellent analysis see Georg Simmel, "The Secret Society," pp. 345-376 in Kurt H. Wolff (ed. and trans.), The Sociology of Georg Simmel. New York: Free Press, 1950, pp. 369-70.

(28) "The San Jose Three, Time 107, #7 (February 16, 1976): 78.

(29) "Ice Cream Maker Charged," Lafayette Journal and Courier (August 7, 1975): A-2.

(30) For a discussion of value rationality see David E. Willer, "Max Weber's Missing Authority Type," Sociological Inquiry 37 (Spring 1967): 231-39.

(31) This distinction is discussed by Friedrich Baerwald, "Humanism and Social Ambivalence, Thought 62, #167 (Winter 1967): 554.

(32) Stanley Weir, "The ILWU: A Case Study in Bureaucracy," pp. 80-94 in Burton Hall (ed.), Autocracy and Insurgency in Organized Labor. New Brunswick: Transaction, 1972, p. 80.

(33) "The San Jose Three," op. cit.

(34) "U.S. Leftists, Ex-spooks Plan Worldwide Anti-CIA Group," Lafayette Journal and Courier (July 29, 1978): A-15.

(35) James Robinson, "Lutheran Schism Gains Momentum," Chicago Tribune (August 17, 1975): section 1, 28.

(36) Ibid.

(37) C. George Benello, "Work Management in Organizations: Paradigms and Possibilities," Humanity and Society 2, #2 (May 1978): 114.

(38) Max Weber, "Bureaucracy," pages 196-244 in H.H. Gerth and C. Wright Mills (eds. and trans.) From Max Weber. New York: Oxford University Press, 1946, p. 233.

(39) See, for example, Carole Pateman, Participation and Democratic Theory, Cambridge: Cambridge University Press, 1970.

(40) Ralph Nader et. al., op. cit., p. 184.

(41) William Hines, "Whistling's Not a Happy Tune," Chicago Sun-Times (May 22, 1978): 16.

(42) Nicholas Wade, "Protection Sought for Satirists and Blowers," Science 182 (December 7, 1973): 1003.

(43) Ann Devroy, "Union Reformers Protest 'Tony Pro' Fund Solicitation," Layatette Journal and Courier (August 9, 1978): A-10.

(44) Ibid.

(45) Nora Ephron, "Academic Gore," Esquire 88, #3 (September 1977): 144.

(46) George Santayana, The Life of Reason. New York: Charles Scribner, 1905.

(47) "Public Directors: A Possible Answer to Corporate Misconduct?" Wall Street Journal 61, #112 (March 23, 1976): 1.

(48) David W. Ewing, Freedom Inside the Organization: Bringing Civil Liberties to the Workplace, New York: E.P. Dutton, 1977.

(49) David W. Ewing, "Let the Employes Cure Corporate Corruption," Chicago Tribune (August 12, 1975): 4.

(50) Jay W. Forrester, quoted in Kenneth D. Walters, op. cit., p. 162.

(51) Thus, it was not until the Congress (and the general public) learned about the fraud, kickbacks and other abuses within the Governmental Services Administration that the G.S.A.'s administrator "publicly reinstated four whistle-blowing employees who had been dismissed or demoted for attempting to publicize G.S.A. wrongdoing." ("Biggest Scandal," Time 112, #11 (September 11, 1978): 22.

Bibliography

"Action Line," Chicago Tribune (April 20, 1976) Section 2, 1.

Agee, Phillip, "Why I Split the C.I.A. and Spilled the Beans," Esquire 83, #6 (June, 1975), 128-30.

"Alexander Butterfield," People Weekly 3, #15 (April 21, 1975), 66.

Anderson, Jack, "AF's Soviet-Style Hush Up," Lafayette Journal and Courier (July 13, 1978), Section A, 8.

Anderson, Stanley V., "Comparing Classical and Executive Ombudsmen," 305-15 in Alan J. Wyner (ed.), Executive Ombudsmen in the United States, Berkley: University of California Press, 1973.

Anstett, Patricia, "Teamster Rebel Leader Launches Reform Campaign," Chicago Sun-Times (September 19, 1977): p. 66.

Aronson, Elliot and Judson Mills, "The Effect of Severity of Initiation on Liking for a Group," Journal of Abnormal and Social Psychology 59 (1959), 117-181.

Atwater, James, "Company Man," Time 106, #5 (August 4, 1975): 62-63.

Baerwald, Friedrich, "Humanism and Social Ambivalence," Thought XLII, #167 (Winter, 1967): 543-60.

Barnard, Chester I., The Functions of the Executive, Cambridge: Harvard University Press, 1938.

Bay, Christian, "Civil Disobedience: Prerequisite for Democracy in Mass Society," 222-42 in Donald W. Hanson and Robert Booth Fowler (eds.), Obligation and Dissent: An Introduction to Politics, Boston: Little, Brown, 1971.

Bayley, David H., "The Effects of Corruption in a Developing Nation," Western Political Quarterly XIX, #4 (December, 1966): 719-32.

"Bell Testimony Tells Procurer Role," Chicago Sun-Times (August 16, 1977): 18.

Benello, C. George, "Work Management in Organizations: Paradigms and Possibilities," Humanity and Society 2, #2 (May, 1978): 104-23.

Benson, J. Kenneth, "Innovation and Crisis in Organizational Analysis," Sociological Quarterly 18, #1 (Winter, 1977): 3-16.

"Biggest Scandal," Time 112, #11 (September 11, 1978): 22.

Blank, Blanche D., "The Battle of Bureaucracy," The Nation 203 (December 12, 1966): 632-36.

Blau, Peter, Exchange and Power in Social Life. New York: Wiley, 1964.

Blau, Peter M. and W. Richard Scott, Formal Organizations: A Comparative Approach. San Francisco: Chandler, 1962.

Brinton, Crane, The Anatomy of Revolution. New York: Vintage, 1957.

Brodie, Bernard, "Strategy." International Encyclopedia of the Social Sciences, Vol. 15. New York: Macmillan, 1968.

Bukro, Casey, "Nuclear Plants: Safety Dispute Mushrooms," Chicago Tribune (February 16, 1976): 1.

"Bureaucracy Tale: Don't Blow Whistle," Chicago Tribune (May 12, 1975): 12.

Cartwright, Dorwin and Alvin Zander (eds.), Group Dynamics: Research and Theory. Evanston, Illinois: Row Peterson, 1953.

"Coal and the UMW are Still at Odds," Business Week #2498 (August 29, 1977): 29.

Cockburn, Alexander, "Agee's Book (as yet) Unbanned," Village Voice (June 16, 1975): 43, 46.

Cockburn, Alexander and James Ridgeway, "Scientist J. Anthony Morris - He Fought the Flu Shots and the U.S. Fired Him," Long Island Press (Parade Magazine) (March 13, 1977): 20,22.

Collins, Randall, Conflict Sociology. New York: Academic Press, 1976.

Cose, Ellis, "The Unlearnable Lesson," Chicago Sun-Times (November 24, 1975): 230.

Coser, Louis, Continuities in the Study of Social Conflict. New York: Free Press, 1967.

Crozier, Michael, The Bureaucratic Phenomenon. Chicago, Ill.: University of Chicago Press, 1964.

Devroy, Ann. "Union Reformers Protest 'Tony Pro' Fund Solicitation," Lafayette Journal and Courier (August 9, 1978): Section A, 10.

Dewar, Helen, "Temporary Halt in Wildcat Strike Ordered by UMW," Washington Post (August 23, 1977): 1, 4.

"Doctor Charges Army Exams Lax," Lafayette Journal and Courier (July 31, 1978): 1.

Douglas, Jack and John M. Johnson (eds.), Official Deviance: Readings in Malfeasance, Misfeasance and Other Forms of Corruption. Philadelphia, Pa.: Lippincott, 1977.

Downton, James V. Rebel Leadership: Commitment and Charisma in the Revolutionary Process. New York: Free Press, 1973.

Durkheim, Emile, The Division of Labor in Society. Glencoe, Ill.: Free Press, 1947.

Duverger, Maurice, "The Two Faces of Janus," 111-114 in Michael A. Weinstein (ed.) The Political Experience: Readings in Political Science. New York: St. Martin's Press, 1972.

Eckstein, Harry (ed.), Internal War: Problems and Approaches. New York: Free Press, 1964.

Eckstein, Harry, "On the Causes of Internal Wars, 287-309 in Eric A. Nordlinger (ed.), Politics and Society: Studies in Comparative Political Sociology, Englewood Cliffs, N.J.: Prentice-Hall, 1970.

Ephron, Nora, "Academic Gore," Esquire 88, #3 (September, 1977): 76 ff.

Ephron, Nora, "The Bennington Affair," Esquire 86, #3 (September, 1976): 53-58, 142-151.

Ermann, M. David and Richard J. Lundman (eds.), Corporate and Governmental Deviance: Problems of Organizational Behavior in Contemporary Society. New York: Oxford University Press, 1978.

Ermann, M. David and Richard J. Lundman, "Deviant Acts by Complex Organizations: Deviance and Social Control at the Organizational Level of Analysis," Sociological Quarterly 19 (Winter, 1978): 55-67.

Evan, William M., "The Inspector General in the U.S. Army," 147-52 in Donald C. Rowat (ed.), The Ombudsman: Citizen's Defender. London: George Allen and Unwin, 1965.

Ewing, David W., Freedom Inside the Organization: Bringing Civil Liberties to the Workplace. New York: E.P. Dutton, 1977.

Ewing, David W., "Let the Employees Cure Corporate Corruption," Chicago Tribune (August 12, 1975): 4.

Finer, S.E. (ed.), Vilfredo Pareto: Sociological Writing. New York: Praeger, 1966.

Frailey, Fred W., "Wildcat Strikes: Preview of Turmoil in Coal Fields," U.S. News and World Report 83, #10 (September 5, 1977): 65-67.

Gall, Peter, "The Culture of Bureaucracy: Mores of Protest," Washington Monthly 2, #4 (June, 1970): 75-83.

Gamson, William A., The Strategy of Social Protest, Homewood, Ill.: Dorsey Press, 1974.

Gerth, H.H. and C. Wright Mills (eds.), From Max Weber: Essays in Sociology, New York: Oxford University Press, 1946.

Ginsberg, Morris, Sociology, London: Oxford University Press, 1953.

Glaser, Barney, "The Local: Cosmopolitan Scientist," American Journal of Sociology 69 (November, 1963): 246-60.

Glass, James M., "Consciousness and Organization: The Disintegration of Joseph K. and Bob Slocum," Administration and Society 7, #3 (November, 1975): 366-83.

Glass, James M., "Realty and Organization: The Executive as Depth Personality Structure," Paper delivered at the Northeast Political Science meetings, Jug End, Massachusetts; November 1976.

Goodman, Paul and Donald R. Van Houten, "Managerial Strategies and the Worker: a Marxist Analysis of Bureaucracy," Sociological Quarterly 18 (Winter, 1977): 108-25.

Gouldner, Alvin W., The Coming Crisis in Western Sociology, New York: Basic Books, 1970.

Gross, Edward, "The Definition of Organizational Goals," British Journal of Sociology XX, #3 (September, 1969): 277-94.

Gurr, Ted Robert, Why Men Rebel, Princeton: Princeton University Press, 1970.

Hall, Burton (ed.), Autocracy and Insurgency in Organized Labor. New Brunswick, New Jersey: Transaction Press, 1972.

Hall, Burton, "Introduction," pp. 1-8 in Burton Hall (ed.), Autocracy and Insurgency in Organized Labor. New Brunswick, N.J.: Transaction Press, 1972.

Halperin, Martin E., et al. The Lawless Crimes of the U.S. Intelligence Agencies. New York: Penguin Books, 1976.

Hanson, Donald W. and Robert Booth Fowler (eds.), Obligation and Dissent: An Introduction to Politics, Boston: Little, Brown, 1971.

Hass, J. Eugene and Thomas E. Drabeck, Complex Organizations: A Sociological Perspective. New York: Macmillan, 1973.

Heller, Joseph, Something Happened. New York: Ballantine, 1975.

Heydebrand, Wolf, "Organizational Contradictions in Public Bureaucracies: Toward A Marxian Theory Of Organizations," Sociological Quarterly 18 (Winter, 1977): 83-107.

Hines, William, "Whistling's Not a Happy Tune," Chicago Sun-Times (May 22, 1978): 16.

Homans, George, Social Behavior. New York: Harcourt, Brace and World, 1961.

Houston, Jack, "Learning How To Get Along With The Boss," Chicago Tribune (August 10, 1975): Section 12, 1.

Hummel, Ralph P., The Bureaucratic Experience. New York: St. Martin's Press, 1977.

"Ice Cream Gate," Time 106, #7 (August 18, 1975): 67.

"Ice Cream Maker Charged," Lafayette Journal and Courier (August 7, 1975): Section A, 2.

Jay, Anthony, Management and Machiavelli: An Inquiry into the Politics of Corporate Life. New York: Bantam Books, 1968.

Jay, Anthony, The Corporation Man. New York: Pocket Books, 1973.

Jones, James, From Here to Eternity. New York: Scribner, 1951.

Josephson, Eric and Mary Josephson (eds.), Man Alone: Alienation in Modern Society. New York: Dell, 1962.

Judith Ann, "The Secretarial Proletariat," 86-100 in Robin Morgan (ed.), Sisterhood is Powerful: An Anthology of Writings from the Women's Movement. New York: Random House, 1970.

Kant, Immanuel, Fundamental Principles of the Metaphysics of Morals. Indianapolis: Bobbs-Merrill, 1949.

Keen, Ernest, Three Faces of Being: Toward an Existentialist Clinical Psychology. New York: Appleton-Century-Crofts, 1970.

Kornhauser, William, "Rebellion and Political Development," 142-56 In Harry Eckstein (ed.), Internal War: Problems and Approaches. New York: Free Press, 1964.

La Boetie, Etienne de, The Politics of Obedience: The Discourse of Voluntary Servitude, New York: Free Life Editions, 1975.

La Velle, Mike, "Shielding Workers From Their Unions," Chicago Tribute (May 26, 1977): Section 3, 4.

Lawrence, John F., "The Mid-Life Crisis: When Male Menopause Joke Isn't Funny," Chicago Sun-Times (July 5, 1977): 45.

Lawrence, Peter A., Georg Simmel: Sociologist and European, New York: Harper and Row, 1976.

Leavitt, Harold J., William R. Dill and Henry B. Eyring, "Rulemakers and Referees," 259-77 in M. David Ermann and Richard J. Lundman (eds.), Corporate and Governmental Deviance: Problems of Organizational Behavior in Contemporary Society. New York: Oxford University Press, 1978.

Lingeman, Richard R. "Book Ends: Secrets, Secrets," New York Times Book Review (May 28, 1978): 27.

Magnuson, Ed, "Expedient Truths," Time 108, #17 (October 25, 1976): 83-84.

Maitland, Leslie, "Story of an East Side Policeman Who Turned in Fellow Officers," New York Times (July 3, 1977): 1, 33.

Mannheim, Karl, Ideology and Utopia. New York: Harcourt, Brace and World, 1936.

Martin, David C., "Probes Reveal Frequent Abuse of Nation's Intelligence Agencies," Indianapolis Star (December 14, 1975): 20.

Marx, Karl, "Alienated Labor," 93-105 in Eric Josephson and Mary Josephson (eds.) Man Alone: Alienation in Modern Society. New York: Dell, 1962.

Mass, Peter, Serpico. New York: Bantam, 1973.

Mechanic, David, "Sources of Power of Lower Participants in Complex Organizations," Administrative Science Quarterly 7, #3 (December, 1962): 349-64.

Merton, Robert K., "Bureaucratic Structure and Personality," Social Forces 18, #4 (May, 1940): 560-68.

Merton, Robert K., "Bureaucratic Structure and Personality," 195-206 in Robert K. Merton (ed.), Social Theory and Social Structure. New York: Free Press, 1957.

Milbrath, Lester, Political Participation: How and Why Do People Get Involved In Politics?. Chicago: Rand McNally, 1965.

Milgram, Stanley, "Professionals in Bureaucracy: Alienation Among Industrial Scientists and Engineers," American Sociological Review 32 (October, 1967): 755-68.

Mills, C. Wright, The Sociological Imagination, New York: Oxford University Press, 1958.

Morgan, Robin (ed.), Sisterhood Is Powerful: An Anthology of Writings from the Women's Movement, New York: Random House, 1970.

"'Ms.' Gazette News," Ms. VII, #1 (July, 1978): 85-88.

Nader, Ralph, Peter J. Petkas and Kate Blackwell (eds.), Whistle Blowing: The Report on the Conference on Professional Responsibility, New York: Grossman Publishers, 1972.

Nandi, Proshanta K., "Career and Life Organization of Professionals: A Study of Contrasts Between College and University Professors," (Ph.D. dissertation, University of Minnesota, 1968).

Nordlinger, Eric A. (ed.), Politics and Society: Studies in Comparative Political Sociology, Englewood Cliffs, N.J.: Prentice Hall, 1970.

Nye, J.S., "Corruption and Political Development: a Cost Benefit Analysis," American Political Science Review LXI, #2 (June, 1967): 417-27.

Olson, Mancur, The Logic of Collective Action, Cambridge: Harvard University Press, 1965.

Page, Joseph A., "What the FDA Won't Tell You About FDS," Washington Monthly 5, #1 (March, 1973): 19-25.

Parsons, Talcott, The Structure of Social Action. Glencoe, Ill.: Free Press, 1949.

Pateman, Carole, Participation and Political Theory, Cambridge: Cambridge University Press, 1970.

Pearre, James, "AMA Sweats Out Case Of 'Sore Throat'," Chicago Tribune (August 17, 1975): 10.

Peter, Laurence J. and Raymond Hull, The Peter Principle. New York: William Morrow, 1969.

Peters, Charles and Taylor Branch, Blowing the Whistle: Dissent in the Public Interest. New York: Praeger, 1972.

Phillips, B.J., "The Case of Karen Silkwood: The Mysterious Death Of A Nuclear Plant Worker," Ms III, #10 (April, 1975): 59-66.

"Phone Calls And Philandering: Ma Bell's Slip Shows in a San Antonio Courtroom," Time 110, #10 (September 5, 1977): 32-33.

"Phone Company Loses Suit," Lafayette Journal and Courier (September 13, 1977): 2.

Porter, Doug and Margaret Van Houten, "CIA As White-Collar Mafia: Marchetti Ungagged," Village Voice (June 16, 1975): 43 ff.

Prescott, Stanley, "Why And How IRS Needs Reforming," Freedom XIX (September/ October, 1974): 3.

Presthus, Robert, The Organizational Society: An Analysis and a Theory, New York: Vintage-Random House, 1962.

"Public Directors: A Possible Answer To Corporate Misconduct," Wall Street Journal 61, #112 (March 23, 1976): 1.

Quinn, Sally, "John Dean: No Tears, Scars," Chicago Sun-Times (October 24, 1976): 4.

Reeves, Richard, "The Last Angry Man," Esquire (March 1, 1978): 41-48.

Rejai, Mostafa, The Strategy of Political Revolution, Garden City, N.Y.: Doubleday, 1973.

Riesman, David, et. al. The Lonely Crowd: A Study of the Changing American Character. Garden City, N.Y.: Doubleday, 1950.

Ringle, William, "Teamsters Find Rebels Growing," Lafayette Journal and Courier (July 31, 1977): Section D, 7.

Robinson, James, "Lutheran Schism Gains Momentum," Chicago Tribune (August 17, 1975): Section 1, 28.

Roethlisberger, F.J. and William J. Dickson, Management and the Worker. Cambridge: Harvard University Press, 1939.

Rothschild, Emma, Paradise Lost: The Decline of the Auto-Industrial Age. New York: Random House, 1973.

Rowat, Donald C., "Introduction," pp. 7-10 in Donald C. Rowat (ed.), The Ombudsman: Citizen's Defender. London: George Allen and Unwin, 1965.

Roy, Donald, "Efficiency and 'The Fix': Informal Intergroup Relations In A Piecework Machine Shop," American Journal of Sociology 60 (1955): 225-66.

Santayana, Georg, The Life of Reason; or, The Phases of Human Progress. New York: Scribners, 1905-1926.

Sartre, Jean Paul, Search for a Method, New York: Random House, 1963.

Schapiro, Leonard, "Trails of a Translator," The New York Times Book Review (August 13, 1978): 13.

Scheff, Thomas J., "Control Over Policy By Attendants in a Mental Hospital," Journal of Health and Human Behavior 2 (1961): 93-105.

Scheler, Max, Ressentiment, New York: Schocken Books, 1961.

Scott, Niki, "Belle Bides Time With Nasty Boss," Chicago Sun-Times (May 1, 1977): 4.

"Secretary As Servant Is Typical," Chicago Tribune (August 14, 1977): 37.

Shils, Edward A. and Morris Janowitz, "Cohesion And Disintegration In The Wehrmacht In World War II," Public Opinion Quarterly 12 (Summer, 1948): 280-315. .

Silver, Isidore, "The Corporate Ombudsman," Harvard Business Review 45 (May/June, 1967): 77-87.

Simmel, Georg, Conflict and the Web of Group Affiliations, Glencoe, Ill.: Free Press, 1955.

Simmel, Georg, "The Secret Society," 345-376 in Kurt H. Wolff (ed. and trans.), The Sociology of Georg Simmel. New York: Free Press, 1950.

Simon, Herbert A., "On The Concept Of Organizational Goal," Administrative Science Quarterly 7, #1 (June, 1964): 1-22.

Singer, Kurt, "The Resolution Of Conflict," Social Research 16, #2 (June, 1949): 230-45.

"'Sore Throat' Attacks," Time (August 18, 1975): 54.

Sprott, W.J.H., Human Groups, Baltimore: Penguin Books, 1958.

Stouffer, Samuel A., et al. The American Soldier Volume 1: Adjustment During Army Life. Princeton: Princeton University Press, 1949.

Strong, James, "Teamster 'Ripoff' Charged: Dissidents Assail 'Sky High' Salaries Paid Union Officials," Chicago Tribune (May 28, 1967): 1, 19.

"Suspicion Gathers Around 'Dr. X'," Chicago Tribune 9 January 12, 1976): 1, 18.

Sutherland, Edward H., White Collar Crime, New York: Holt, Rinehart and Winston, 1961.

"The San Jose Three," Time 107, #7 (February 16, 1976): 78.

"The Silkwood Mystery," Time 105, #3 (January 20, 1975): 47-48.

Thompson, Victor A., Modern Organization, New York: Knopf, 1961.

Timnick, Lois, "Twisted Power-Sex Drive Leads VIP Downfall," Chicago Daily News (June 3, 1977): 2.

Tomlinson, Kenneth Y., "The Lonely Ordeal Of Dale Richardson," Reader's Digest 106 (May, 1975): 124-28.

"Union Muscle Flexes Far Beyond Numbers," U.S. News and World Report (May 1, 1978): 57-59.

United States Senate Committee On Governmental Affairs, The Whistle-blowers: A Report on Federal Employees Who Disclose Acts of Governmental Waste, Abuse and Corruption, Washington, D.C.: U.S. Printing Office, February, 1978.

vonHoffman, Nicholas, "Witness For The Betrayal," Chicago Tribune (November 25, 1975): Section 2, 4.

Wade, Nicholas, "Protection Sought For Satirists And Blowers," Science 182 (December 7, 1973): 1002-3.

Walters, Kenneth D.,"Your Employee's Right To Blow The Whistle," Harvard Business Review 53, #4 (July/August, 1975): 26 ff.

Warriner, Charles K., "The Problems Of Organizational Purpose," Sociological Quarterly 6, #2 (Spring, 1965): 139-46.

Weber, Max, "Bureaucracy," 196-244 in H.H. Gerth and C. Wright Mills (eds.), From Max Weber: Essays in Sociology, New York: Oxford University Press, 1946.

Weber, Max, "Politics as a Vocation," 77-128 in H.H. Gerth and C. Wright Mills (Eds.), From Max Weber: Essays in Sociology, New York: Oxford University Press, 1946.

Weber, Max, "The Social Psychology Of The World Religions," 267-301 in H.H. Gerth and C. Wright Mills (eds.), From Max Weber: Essays in Sociology. New York: Oxford University Press, 1946.

Weinstein, Deena and Michael A. Weinstein, Roles of Man: An Introduction to the Social Sciences, Hinsdale, Ill.: Dryden Press, 1972.

Weinstein, Michael A., "Against Human Nature," Paper delivered at the Mid-west Political Science Association meetings, Chicago, Illinois, 1974.

Weinstein, Michael A. (ed.), The Political Experience: Readings in Political Science, New York: St. Martin's Press, 1972.

Weir, Stanley, "The ILWU: A Case Study In Bureaucracy," 80-94 in Burton Hall (ed.), Autocracy and Insurgency in Organized Labor. New Brunswick: Transaction, 1972.

Wenglinsky, Martin, "Review Of Milgram: Obedience To Authority," Contemporary Sociology: A Journal of Reviews 4 (November, 1975): 613-17.

White, Ralph and Ronald Lippitt, "Leader Behavior And Member Reaction In Three 'Social Climates', 585-611 in Dorwin Cartwright and Alvin Zander (eds.), Group Dynamics: Research and Theory. Evanston, Ill.: Row Peterson, 1953.

Willer, David E., "Max Weber's Missing Authority Type," Sociological Inquiry 37 (Spring, 1967): 231-39.

Wolff, Kurt (ed. and trans.), The Sociology of Georg Simmel. New York: Free Press, 1950.

"Worker Kills Boss, Self," The Purdue Exponent 94, #115 (September 12, 1978): 2.

Wyner, Alan J. (ed.), Executive Ombudsmen in the United States. Berkeley: University of California Press, 1973.

Index

About the Author

DEENA WEINSTEIN is Associate Professor of Sociology at DePaul University, Chicago. She is the author of four works on general sociology, including Living Sociology, and more than 17 published scholarly articles in the areas of social philosophy, sociological theory, the sociology of knowledge, the sociology of science, and complex organizations. She serves on the editorial boards of several scholarly journals and has held offices in professional associations.

Pergamon Policy Studies